BIRCHISM
WAS MY BUSINESS

BIRCHISM
WAS MY BUSINESS

Gerald Schomp

THE MACMILLAN COMPANY
COLLIER-MACMILLAN LIMITED, LONDON

The Macmillan Company
866 Third Avenue, New York, N.Y. 10022
Collier-Macmillan Canada Ltd., Toronto, Ontario

Library of Congress Catalog Card Number: 71–120343

First Printing

Printed in the United States of America

This book is dedicated to Tom, a courageous publicity man who accepted the most difficult and frustrating challenge in the history of public relations—trying to improve the public image of Robert Welch and the John Birch Society.

Contents

BIRCHISM
WAS MY BUSINESS

1

The Man from John Birch

For over two years I was a paid, professional patriot for the John Birch Society. I have had some interesting experiences, to say the least. The Society has undoubtedly been one of the most cussed and discussed organizations in the United States. I found it to be one of the most hilarious and, at the same time, one of the most tragic aspects of the American scene.

This book is the first public critique written by someone who has been intimately acquainted with the Society on a sympathetic basis, has helped promote all the Birch programs on a professional level, and personally knows many of the Birch leaders and a sizable cross section of its hidden membership. I believe that my early objective and familiar association with the Birch Society qualifies me as one of its fairest and most knowledgeable critics.

For the most part, however, this book is about me. It is the story of an educated, ambitious, rebellious, slightly spoiled 27-year-old man who allows himself to be trapped into compromising with a simplistic view of all the problems of this great land. It's the story of self-deception and rationalization; disillusionment and confrontation; meditation, realization and atonement. It's the story of gullible Gerald Schomp—a man who made a damn fool out of himself by wildly waving our star-spangled flag in everybody else's face before he even knew what America was all about.

I often wonder now, years later, whatever possessed me to rush pell-mell into the John Birch Society and then throw aside a promising career in communications to join the staff of this highly controversial and widely denounced right-wing organization.

At the time my rationalizations were simple enough. Above all I hated Communism. Having read a considerable number of books about Communist atrocities written by refugees who had escaped from tyranny behind the Iron Curtain, it seemed noble to join any available action group that promised to reveal and revenge Red injustice.

Also, as I am a practicing Catholic, the atheistic basis of the Communist ideology was entirely repugnant to me. Fighting Communism seemed to be a useful and exciting way to practice my religion. It was something interesting that I could do for country and God. Both anti-Communism and Birchism have sacrificial aspects which satisfy idealistic yearnings and help offer meaning to one's existence.

As I look back on it now, however, there are other more subtle—yet infinitely more genuine—reasons why I chose to turn my life around and play cowboys and Indians with imagined conspiracies and fancied threats.

During 1964 and 1965 I was employed by WSUN-TV and Radio in St. Petersburg, Florida. I was listed on employee records as a copywriter and paid accordingly. Actually, however, I was serving in the capacity of public relations director of the station and was recognized as such by associates and business contacts. I had accepted this position as a means to move my family to paradise in Florida and to gain television and radio experience in order to round out my general background in advertising and journalism.

The job, though beneficial to my practical education, was boring and disillusioning. The people I worked with —salesmen, disc jockeys, newsmen, businessmen— seemed stereotyped and empty and hopelessly caught up in pursuit of the American dream called "success" and "respectability." If they personified what I was headed for, I wanted no part of it.

I'm old enough and responsible enough not to be a hippie. But I'm young enough not to have been molded by depression and war, and amply idealistic to want to search for and find meaning for life and creation. My job had nothing to offer in this respect.

I did what I was told, often knowing that what I was told was stupid and self-serving for the people for whom I worked. It made little difference whether I did my work poorly or well. Nobody would notice or care anyway.

It made no difference when I offered suggestions and fresh ideas that I knew would improve the product offered to the public on what is now rightly termed the "boob tube." Things would continue to be done exactly the same way they had always been done. Business was going well. Why monkey with success? It was discouraging to know that my future was directly related to my willingness to submerge myself into the system and serve it slavishly without making anyone nervous.

Was this to be the pattern of my life? Was this why I had worked six years in college? Was it the American dream to trade individuality for conformity, self-satisfaction for security, purpose and dedication for the safety of meaninglessness?

This was not for me. Yet, how could I escape the attitudinal plague that ravishes American creativity and self-expression? How could I keep from being swallowed up in anonymity and digested and excreted in mediocrity?

There had to be a way to assert myself. There had to be a way to tell the world all the things I had to say to it, to do all the stimulating and fulfilling things that might make life worthwhile, to find and fulfill whatever worthy purposes might have been intended for me.

The man in the grey flannel suit was a devil in disguise. The American dream was a nightmare. Success according to acceptable standards was a fraud. Happiness among the middle class was self-deception. Accommodation with the "system"—the "Establishment"—was narcotic, destructive and self-betraying.

I desperately wanted to escape the bleak future that seemed so inevitable. I did not want to be just another face in the crowd. I could not tolerate the thought that I could always be counted upon—by anybody for anything. I did not want to be predictable, absolutely reliable, consistently sensible, compatible with all generally accepted standards of conduct and thought. I did not want to be taken for granted, to be tolerated, to be patronized and accepted in the usually acceptable ways. I began to search desperately for a way to escape the innocuous workaday existence that dominates most people's lives.

Still, I had a family to support. Some kind of job was necessary while I continued to search for an answer to unfulfilled dreams of self-realization, fame and influence. If I was to make my days meaningful, it would have to be on my own time—at least temporarily. It was this quest for some form of expression and fulfillment that led me into right-wing politics and anti-Communism.

I had been a long-time staunch political conservative and this had much to do with my becoming a professional patriot. It was as though extremism were an occupational hazard and I just fell into it, as a zoo keeper might fall into a snake pit.

Conservatism was part of my nature. I was in love with "Mr. Conservative," the late Senator Robert A. Taft, before I was old enough to know what he stood for. By the presidential election of 1964, I was campaigning relentlessly on the premise that White America had gone Pink and was about to become Red unless Senator Barry Goldwater became our next leader.

Goldwater was everything that personifies "goodness" to a conservative—honest, ruggedly articulate, recklessly outspoken, uncompromising in his dealings and absolutely convinced that the American way is always and everywhere the divine way as well.

As I campaigned for Barry, as the doors were politely closed in my face, as elderly people refused to listen because they thought he would take away Social Security, as I watched the atom bomb TV commercial the Democrats used to throw a nuclear smokescreen over the issues, I died a thousand deaths of defeat and despair for my country's Hope as he was crucified at the polls.

At that point, the normal channels for political action seemed totally inadequate. Something more drastic was needed to save America from Communism. Almost immediately I found something more drastic—the John Birch Society. At that time the Society was cringing in the spotlight of national denunciation, but still swelling with great numbers of the disenchanted and the self-disenfranchised right-wing element in America. If the Establishment was that much against it, I reasoned, the Birch Society couldn't be all bad.

I can easily remember the first Birch meeting I ever attended. It was a stimulating experience. I was nervous about meeting with a roomful of radicals, and then encouraged to find that they are quite normal people. The press had led me to expect gritty old women in tennis shoes, beady-eyed students with designs of intrigue and grease-pitted Neanderthals.

Instead, I found ministers disgusted with the social gospel, doctors alarmed over Medicare, mothers concerned about schools and safe streets, businessmen worried about taxes and property values and teachers distraught over permissiveness. Yet, the mystery, adventure, and atmosphere of underground secrecy is definitely there. Although these things are more imagined than real, planning to impeach Earl Warren, to get the "U.S. out of the UN," and to expose the civil rights movement as a Communist plot seems pleasurably naughty—but immeasurably noble. It is closely akin, I believe, to the rationalizations of a Communist Party functionary who dreams of blowing up factories and sabotaging passenger trains all for the sake of glorious Humanity.

Introducing yourself to other skittish first-timers at a Birch meeting is a touchy thing. You can never be sure your boss, or a neighbor, or a school chum won't be there or, worse yet, a business competitor. Short of that small catastrophe, someone just might recognize your name. You can visualize how it will be at the office next day when the word gets around that you're one of those extremist hate-mongers in that organization they're always talking about on TV.

It's a relief when the chitchat is cut off and the business begins. A facetious comment about the FBI writing down the license plate numbers of cars parked outside relieves the tension. Forced chuckles help everyone to relax.

You're told things a suspicious person can readily agree with. America's going to pot. They're just messing around in Vietnam. The politicians are afraid of the punks rioting in the streets. Unions are getting way out of hand. Too many deadbeats leeching off us hard-working people. Supreme Court is atheistic. Taxes will ruin us. Police being persecuted. Communists in State Department. Crime soaring. Drugs rampant. Too much sex. Corruption. Immorality. Propaganda. Anarchy. Pretty soon it dawns on you: sounds sensible to me. They're absolutely right. By golly, these are my people!

Joining the Birch Society was rather easy for me. I knew something about socialism and communism. I

asked intelligent questions and acted hesitant and skepti-
cal. Then the unheard-of happened. At my very first
meeting the man in charge offered me the opportunity to
become the leader of a whole new chapter of Birchers.
The old members were flabbergasted and visibly shocked.
It wasn't a very conservative thing to do. I was delighted
—exhilarated—by the sudden, unexpected recognition of
what I felt were my latent leadership potentialities.

The grey flannel Che Guevara in me clamored to be
free. Adventure over security. Heroism over conformity.
Sacrifice over stability. My country. Red, white, and blue.
Sock it to me, Uncle Sam. Me, the leader . . . The Patriot!

Simple as that, I became a chapter leader of the John
Birch Society in St. Petersburg, Florida. As the captain of
a little team of dedicated, middle-class, counterrevo-
lutionaries, I soon had all the local patriots in staid St.
Petersburg working feverishly to flood the city with
16,000 pieces of mail to refute a newspaper's charge that
the Birch Society was a paramilitary organization that
planned to come out shooting to get revenge for the
Goldwater debacle.

The publication we were mailing was a Birch brochure
headlined "What's Wrong With the American Press—Example No. 1: the St. Petersburg *Times.*" It condemned a
front page news story published by the *Times* just a few
days before the election which was headlined: "St. Petersburg Birchers Told to Arm Selves, Buy Guns for Children." The *Times* had also run a long editorial in the next
day's edition which screamed hysterically in boldface
type, "This is anarchy. This is preparation for resort to
force and violence. It is, in short, outright subversion."

18

Quite naturally, the leaders of the Birch Society were exceedingly disturbed at this thrust at their public relations campaign to project an image of the Society as a legitimate, responsible, anti-Communist educational movement. All they could get out of their St. Petersburg members concerning the cause of the scandalous affair was that at a recent meeting an elderly female member had exhibited a piece of radical literature published by a paramilitary rightist group which might have been seen by a guest, who might have been a reporter, who might have infiltrated the meeting. In any event, Robert Welch —founder and head of the John Birch Society—was furious and threatened to sue. When the *Times* printed his telegrammed answer, but neither retracted nor apologized for the articles, Welch decided to match the paper's circulation by distributing a folder that would set the matter straight.

The Birchers in St. Petersburg weren't quite up to the challenge. Most of the meager membership of all the other chapters in St. Pete were, indeed, little old ladies— the kind who wouldn't dream of being caught wearing anything as modern as tennis shoes. Their greatest difficulty was staying awake at meetings. None of them was the gun-toting type the *Times* had conjured up.

Enter from stage right—General Schomp, boy organizer. In no time at all my small home was brimming with 16,000 folders, envelopes, stamps, string, cartons and a lot of strange-thinking people. Bob Welch was delighted with all this activity. He was so delighted, in fact, that he did not charge us for the folders—a significant concession from the Birch Society.

The little old ladies were not so delighted. Their fingers

were worked down to the bones. When the project was completed and we sought out clues to our success from mailmen, paper boys and printed comments from the *Times* itself, the husband of one of our elderly members wagged his finger in my face and snarled, "Young man, don't you ever do this to us again." As it turned out, our members in St. Pete were readers and talkers, not doers.

All that initial activity from our sleepy little chapters in the retirement center of St. Petersburg attracted attention at the Society headquarters in Belmont, Massachusetts, and prompted a job offer as state coordinator for the John Birch Society. These were the things which went through my mind as I waited for the man from John Birch who would interview me and later decide that I should be a paid Birch organizer.

I think I was a little disappointed when he finally showed up. He was young, tall, soft-spoken, thoroughly Southern, suitably moralistic, thoroughly trained, completely composed, interested, but noncommittal. I offered him iced tea instead of a drink to emphasize my "sensible" living. He scrutinized my bookcase to size up my literary tastes. We went over my background. He was pleased with my master's degree in history—good credentials. My experience in public relations work was practical and valuable. Experience in teaching—useful for public speaking. Leader in college—helpful in organizing people. President of Young Republicans—respectable. Editor of college newspaper—would be a good correspondence man. Family man—responsible. Religious —trustworthy and honest. Good grades and honors—reliable. No special weaknesses that would take up his time in a long training period. We could easily be friends. I would be easy for him to manage. By the time he left I knew I had the job.

I didn't spend much time wondering if I should take it when the job was formally offered. I immediately resigned my position with WSUN-TV-Radio. Rumors about me were quickly transmitted throughout the station.

People hung back. Finally a bold one generated the courage to ask me about my new work. I explained patiently and sincerely and somewhat apologetically that I had found it necessary to leave the safety of the good old publicity department in order to work tirelessly for the preservation of everything wonderful and pure from the insidious advances of the international Communist conspiracy. He looked at me strangely, as if waiting for the punch line. Finally he mumbled something like: "Uh hmmm . . . well, I hope you find what you're looking for." Then he excused himself from my presence.

When the shock and clamor of the others subsided, my former friends didn't know whether to hang their heads in shame, have a good laugh at my expense, or cover my resignation as a sensational, local-boy-gone-bad news story.

My best friend at the station continued to eat lunch with me for my remaining two weeks. But we didn't leave the station together anymore. He always had a reason to meet me somewhere downtown in a small restaurant. He also made it well known around the station that he was a Democrat—a very liberal one. Nobody gave a going-away party for me. When my day of departure came, the staff sent over a secretary with a small, simply inscribed gift. It said, "Best Wishes in Whatever You Do." I was beginning to wonder myself just what it was that I was going to do.

When the word of my new position went out across the land, I attained immediate notoriety. Newspapers and television stations called from all over the state. Reporters were interested in anything I had to say—on any subject. They had never before been able to find a live Bircher, let alone one who would actually be willing to talk to them for publication. Mind you, this was before I even had a chance to call anyone a Communist. Would-be Birch members wrote strange notes setting up clandestine meetings so they might persuade me that they had unusual weapons for fighting the Communist conspiracy. One student phoned and whispered that I should call him back tomorrow. "And if my mother answers," he continued, "be sure to tell her you're one of my teachers." He forgot to tell me his name or his telephone number.

I guess all this commotion was what I had really wanted. Instant recognition. Instant power. An instant chance to thumb my nose at society and back it up with the anonymous activity of perhaps a thousand nameless, dedicated workers. The Establishment feared the organized, efficient tentacles of this stealthy organization. They couldn't see the Society—or control it—or even reason with it. I aimed to play upon that fear. I began to have one hell of a good time.

The Birch Society was the right place to exploit fear, curiosity, sensationalism and mystery. It is the only national, permanently-organized, grass-roots organization set up to effectively marshal right-wing forces in the United States. It has a staff of approximately 250 employees, full-time public relations men who run themselves ragged trying to take the tarnish off the Society's image, a permanent recruiting program that uses the latest techniques in printed and audio-visual aids, and continued financial support that enables the organization to work in a first-class manner.

The Society publishes two slick magazines: *American Opinion,* the highly profitable monthly, and *Review of the News,* a weekly with a small circulation which has cost the Society a bundle of money to maintain. It also has a large book publishing operation, Western Islands, which turns out right-wing books and pamphlets by the hundreds. Members of the Society now operate over 400 bookstores, most of them very small outlets that sell under the name American Opinion Libraries. The Society calls it the largest chain of bookstores in the country.

They also claim that the American Opinion Speakers Bureau is the most active in the world. From my observations, it is certainly the most abusive. The Society's 15-minute radio program called "Are You Listening Uncle Sam?" was a big bust and has been replaced with a series of taped Birch commercials available to any member who has enough nerve and money to put them on the air.

For members who have a questioning mind (unfortunately there aren't many), the Society maintains a tiny research bureau which exists mainly in the memory cells of Dr. Francis X. Gannon, Robert Welch's walking encyclopedia. In addition, the Society has an ever-growing variety of records, tapes, films, posters, petitions, bumper stickers, post cards, prepared newspaper ads and other gimmicks that enable its membership to assault the public with the Birch message in every conceivable way.

Growth of the Society was fantastic until early 1965,

especially when you consider what a person has to endure when he becomes a member. From the little band of
wealthy businessmen who met with Robert Welch in
Indianapolis on December 9, 1958 to found the Society, it
has grown to an organization that claims from 60,000 to
100,000 members. Former top staff members, however,
estimate there are now about 25,000 members on the
rolls who regularly attend meetings and actively participate in some of the prescribed projects.

The local members are grouped into chapters of from
seven to twenty-five people under the direction of a chapter leader. The chapter leader is supervised by a section
leader, who in turn reports to a paid coordinator. Those
who do not wish to associate with the local members, or
are too timid to do so, are put into the Home Chapter.
They communicate with and pay dues directly to the
national office. Dues are $24 per year for men and $12
for women and students. All members are strongly urged
to follow their monthly John Birch *Bulletin* and to work
on a relatively standard agenda which includes: increasing the reach of Society publications, speakers, and
bookstores; recruiting more members; and working toward impeaching Earl Warren and the rest of the Supreme Court, getting the U.S. out of the UN, winning the
war in Vietnam, attacking the civil rights movement,
supporting local police and abolishing the income tax.
Raising more and more money in smaller and smaller
amounts has become increasingly important in recent
years as the biggest single sources of large donations
have one by one parted company with Mr. Welch.

Birchers are prolific letter writers and the Society has
launched over 200 letter-writing campaigns aimed at ac-

24

complishing everything from persuading airlines to put conservative publications on the reading racks of their planes to congratulating top Mormon Church officials for making speeches partial to John Birch Society programs. Birchers also do much of their work through thousands of local ad hoc committees, or front organizations, set up to enable non-Birchers to assist on a particular project without swallowing the entire Birch program.

The Birch Society is a monolithic organization. Important decisions are made at the top by Robert Welch who is sometimes assisted by his Council of advisers who meet every three months and stamp Welch's decisions with their seal of approval. Nobody joins the Society in order to participate in the democratic decision-making processes. A person ideally becomes a Bircher only because he is in basic agreement with the established programs and wants to go to work to help carry them out. In this respect, Robert Welch likes to compare the JBS to the Catholic Church. The similarity ends there.

2

Robert Welch—
The Makings of a Radical

When writing human interest stories it is traditional to reveal a heart of gold under the thick skin of every unloved public figure. Ruthless business tycoons quietly give millions to widows and orphans. Pimps and prostitutes give conscience money to Little Sisters of the Poor. Boxers, bouncers, buxom bunnies and the men on death row love little children and crippled animals.

The well of human kindness doesn't run dry for professional patriots, either. Once you get to know us all kinds of lovable little traits bubble up to the surface and make it difficult to concentrate on the fallacies of our philosophy. So it is with the most successful right-wing extremist of them all.

Curious people ask many questions about the John Birch Society: Who founded it? Who determines its strategy? Who controls it? The answer is always the same: Robert Welch. To know Robert Welch is not necessarily to love him. But to know him is to know what the Birch Society is really like. As Welch goes, so goes the Society.

In appearance, Mr. Welch resembles the cartoon character Mr. Magoo. He looks quite harmless and fatherly. If Welch were ringing a bell for the Salvation Army at Christmas, you'd want to give him a dollar.

It's a different story when you scrutinize Welch under pressure. As the heat builds up he lets off steam like a temperamental opera star. Welch is especially irritated by the press, which he feels has become the unwitting propaganda arm for the Communist International. Whenever reporters get within shouting distance of him, they invariably want answers for the same old embarrassing questions which Welch won't and can't answer satisfactorily. Questions like:

Do you still think President Eisenhower was a Communist?

Why don't you make the names of your members public?

Do you really think 90 per cent of our government is Communist controlled?

Welch's relations with the press have been so bad that in recent years he has rarely allowed himself to be interviewed.

Of course, Welch will not admit to being an extremist —unless it is conceded that George Washington, Thomas Jefferson and Paul Revere were also extremists. (All Birchers, in fact, fancy themselves to be patriots in the colonial tradition. They frequently don Revolutionary

27

War costumes and ride on floats for Independence Day parades.) According to Welch he's in the mainstream of traditional American thinking. The real extremists in America are people like Chet Huntley, the Rockefeller brothers, the Smothers brothers and the leading ladies of the national PTA. Welch figures he's all right; it's the rest of the world that's gone wrong.

Welch is small in stature, large in ambition; short on tolerance and long on convictions. He provides comic relief for anyone who doesn't take him seriously. Welch, however, takes himself very seriously. Strong-willed in every way, he is dogmatic on every subject and impatient with anybody who disagrees. As he put it in his *Blue Book:** "The men who join the John Birch Society during the next few months or few years are going to be doing so primarily because they believe in me and what I'm doing and are willing to accept my leadership anyway." Amen.

Over the years most of the members and many staff members have privately disagreed with much that Welch does; but for some reason they accept his leadership anyway. I did it myself, but can't explain why.

Welch rules with an iron fist and has outsmarted every heretic who tried to make him step down as the Society's administrative head. Still, Welch insists he wishes to be remembered by posterity only as the Society's founding father (a dubious distinction, to be sure).

I met the incredible Robert Welch when he came to Florida as the main attraction for a fund-raising drive which I arranged. I had heard so many of our more

* The printed transcript of the speech Robert Welch gave at the Society's founding meeting in December, 1958. It is still the Society's bible.

28

fanatical members rave about his superstamina and super intelligence that I was terribly disappointed when he proved to be another mere mortal. His first half hour with me consisted entirely of a nervous, staccato litany of complaints about his lack of sleep, the last town he was in where parties were arranged for him far into the night, and the incompetent nincompoops who surrounded him at the home office.

Later, when we entered the National Guard Armory in Ft. Lauderdale for his speech, no one even recognized Mr. Welch. It seemed appropriate that the door was decorated with a large angry eagle. Welch was angry himself because I had just informed him that it was arranged that he would talk privately with local leaders and large contributors in a side room before his main address.

As if to penalize us for this inconvenience (which had been requested by his own top level staff), Welch would not allow anyone to open any windows or turn on fans to cool the small, closed room. For thirty minutes 200 people sweltered through a heated discussion on how to support our national patriot—Robert Welch.*

Welch cheered up a bit when he saw the size of the crowd that was filling up the Armory outside the meeting room. We had rigged the seating arrangement so that we would have an overflow crowd no matter how many showed up. The organized confusion was most impressive for the press as the police cleared the crowded side aisles in order to pull portable bleachers down from the

---

* The only cool one in the crowd was a tricky reporter who managed to sneak into the closely guarded room to get an inside story. He got one. The next day papers all over the country told of Welch's approval of a "plot" to take over the board of directors of the CBS television network by buying up their stock.

29

walls to accommodate the overflow. It took weeks of work to turn this audience out and outdraw Martin Luther King who was speaking in nearby Miami the same night. We bussed Birchers in from the other coast of Florida and hundreds drove as much as 500 miles to be on hand for the great gathering of the clan.

I had charge of the program for the evening. The introductions were mine, the mayor of Ft. Lauderdale having unhesitatingly declined the honor. As I stood before the huge crowd drunk with power and the drama of the moment—coming as it did during the congressional elections when Birch extremism was a national issue—I was nearly overcome by a tremendous urge to make sensational news by introducing Welch with an earth-shattering proclamation:

Fellow right-wing extremists. This old man standing on my right is the famous Robert Welch, founder of the notorious John Birch Society. It gives me rare pleasure to tell you a little bit about him. Robert Welch is the man who says our former president, Dwight David Eisenhower, was a Communist agent. He is the man who says the movement to give the American Negro his civil rights is a Communist plot . . . the man who wants to impeach Earl Warren . . . the man who says our government is deliberately fighting the war in Vietnam in order to help the Communist conspiracy. Fellow extremists, I give you Robert Welch. I give him to you because personally I can't stand him any longer.

The odd thing about this introduction—if I had given it—is that Robert Welch would not have heard a word of it. The sound was fine throughout the auditorium except for the first three rows which were behind the overhanging speakers. The people in front, including Welch, couldn't hear clearly. Welch would simply have come on stage, as he did, with his normal three-hour reading of excerpts from one of his own pamphlets (this one was *A Touch of Sanity*) while 1,600 people grumbled, scratched and perspired profusely in a non-air-conditioned sweatbox of a gymnasium designed for close-order drilling.

Mr. Welch strayed once—only once—and looked up from his reading to bawl out a photographer who was maneuvering into position to take a picture and stealing attention from him. When the ordeal was over, Mr. Welch instructed everyone to line up to the right (always to the right!) in order to meet him and get copies of the *Blue Book* autographed.

On the plus side, there's no doubt about Welch's personal courage. Who else in his situation would go to Howard University, a Negro school, to try to convince a hostile black audience that they were being used as tools of the Communists? Welch also agreed to go to the University of California at Berkeley to lecture on how the United States should use all means necessary to win a quick military victory in Vietnam. In the latter part of 1969 Welch embarked on an extensive speaking tour of college campuses. His reception was frequently less than gracious, but Welch never lets giggles, hecklers, catcalls or jeers deter his mission of saving America from other Americans.

At Birch headquarters in Belmont Robert Welch is a perpetual motion machine despite the fact that he's now in his seventies. He works long hours, sometimes writing leaflets far into the night. Occasionally he sleeps on a couch in his office and greets his staff in the morning in a rumpled suit and full day's growth of beard.

Welch has pointed out that he has written 1,200,000 words for the first 100 Birch *Bulletins.* He explained with his typically corny humor: " 'Many have died,' I told my wife proudly, 'from writing that much every month.' 'Yes,' she replied, 'and others have been shot.' "

Welch's writing style is easily identified. He has an exceptional knack for injecting a fatherly personality into his monthly *Bulletins* and books. This has been one of the secrets of his success in winning such a blind and unwavering dedication from the rank and file Birch membership. Almost all Birchers feel that they know Robert Welch like an old friend, even though most have never met him.

Welch also has a number of books and booklets to his credit, or discredit, as the case may be. Some of them were prepared by ghostwriters. The voluminous footnotes for *The Politician,* his controversial book about President Eisenhower, were written by his researcher, Dr. Gannon, to give an aura of scholarship to the work. One of his booklets, *On the Shape of Things to Come,* was published under the name of Chester Berrlow (a scramble of all the letters in "Robert R. Welch") so that sensitive Birchers could approach their friends with literature that did not bear the stigma of either the Society or Welch's name.

This problem of not owning up to being a Bircher poses a dilemma for staff organizers working directly with the membership. I can fully understand their reluctance to announce to the world that they are right-wing

32

extremists. I was often reluctant to reveal it myself, even though I was financially secure on the Birch payroll.

I dreaded my responsibility to call on business concerns during the day in order to "discover" latent conservatives who might give financial aid to JBS activities. Invariably, when I called on a shopkeeper or a manager he would suspiciously demand that I state my business on the spot rather than go to his private office to talk. This was always followed on my part by a gulp and the devastating introduction, "My name is Jerry Schomp and I'm a coordinator for the John Birch Society."

A look of horror would cross his face as customers and employees stopped in their tracks and turned around to see the spectacle, much like people dash into the street when they hear screeching tires followed by a loud crash. The next reaction from my potential patron would be something like, "My God, man! Are you trying to ruin me?"

Noting that it was hardly the time to sell him a *Blue Book* and slip him an application blank, I would beat a hasty retreat, smiling awkwardly at the open-mouthed spectators as I left in abject humiliation as though I was being drummed out of the store.

Once I traipsed into a newspaper office and announced loudly, "Hi there, I'm from the John Birch Society." A perky little squab of a secretary retorted, "The devil ye are!" and everyone gathered around to hear my story.

While the world may wonder about Welch's sanity, no one can deny that he has a certain genius for organization. Few people could hold together a precarious body of independent cusses, weather an unprecedented barrage of damaging publicity and survive internal dissension

33

that would blow apart any other type of organizational structure. Most of his followers attribute Welch's success to his former record as a student and a businessman.

Robert Welch was born on December 1, 1899 on a farm in Chowan County, North Carolina. Many of his ancestors were farmers and Baptist preachers. As the story is told (and the story is told often), young Welch read the entire nine volumes of Ridpath's *History of the World* by the time he was seven years old. The rest of the legend is glossed over rapidly: enrolled at University of North Carolina at age 12. Graduated at age 17. Attended Annapolis for two years where he led his class. Attended Harvard Law School for two years and received top marks. Joined his brother's candy manufacturing business. Did a lot of leading there; also made a modest fortune. Had a brief fling into politics in 1950 when he ran for lieutenant governor of Massachusetts with the U.S. Constitution as his platform. Was trounced. As he reportedly put it later, "The Divine Savior Himself couldn't get elected to office in Massachusetts running as a conservative." Realized his destiny was to save America from the stupidity of the Communist conspiracy and the voting public. Got out of candy business. Got into patriotism business. Made good there, too.

Welch founded the Birch Society in 1958 when he explained his plans to business friends meeting in Indianapolis. He named his organization after Captain John Birch, a Baptist missionary who had served behind enemy lines in China during World War II. As Welch had explained in his book, *The Life of John Birch,* the missionary had been shot and bayonetted to death by Chinese Communists ten days after the end of the war.

34

Welch claimed this made the captain America's first known casualty of the cold war.

The early days of the Society were without due controversy. *National Review* commented: "There is no question that he has stirred the slumbering spirit of patriotism in thousands of Americans, roused them from lethargy, and changed their apathy into a deep desire to learn the facts about Communism and then implement that knowledge with effective and responsible action."

National Review and its editor, William Buckley, haven't had a kind word for Welch since then. Buckley believes that Welch's antics are destroying the conservative movement. Welch strongly implies that Buckley is a Trojan horse leading the right wing onto tangents to help make the world safe for Communism. In a way perhaps they deserve each other.

Many critics wonder what possesses Robert Welch when he makes fantastic generalizations that even embarrass most Birchers. Some think he does it for publicity. Others believe he uses controversy to arouse curiosity for recruiting purposes. Tom Anderson, farm magazine publisher and member of the Birch Council, excuses Welch's conclusions about Eisenhower as an inability to comprehend that a national leader could possibly make mistakes without sinister motivations.

In my opinion Welch's biggest problem is a serious defect in his powers of logic. Perhaps he's just too impatient to weigh all the facts carefully before forming judgments. Repeatedly, he seems to make up his mind on matters through some sort of intuition—and *then* searches for facts to bear out his conclusions. I call it "Welchian logic."

35

Once, at a recruiting presentation, I heard a clever prospect use Welchian logic to "prove" that Robert Welch was a Communist. Enraged Birchers bounced up and down in their chairs like they hadn't been properly toilet trained while he went on and on citing instances of how Birch policies could be helping the Communists. I was too fascinated to try to stop the speaker. The others couldn't.

The most disastrous mistake Welch ever made was writing a very long letter about Dwight Eisenhower which the press picked up and used against him and the Society. Rather than retract the whole thing and save what was left of his prestige, Welch felt compelled to publish it as a book—*The Politician.*

Birchers have a terrible time explaining away his absurd position. Very few members or employees actually believe that President Eisenhower was a Communist. And believe me, they are all fully aware that *The Politician* has kept more people away from the Society than any other single factor. Stubborn as ever, Welch insists that the JBS continue to use *The Politician* as a recruiting weapon.

If you ever meet a Bircher, throw it up to him some time. "Say, Mr. Jones, did Robert Welch really call good ol' Ike a Communist?" Notice the nervous smile and the deep breath before he strikes a nonchalant pose and tries to talk his way out of it.

There are three alternative responses open to Mr. Jones, none of them good. He can insist that Robert Welch never called Eisenhower a Communist. (He did.) *[He was]* He can argue that he agrees with Welch completely that Eisenhower was a Communist (not very good public rela-

36

tions). Or, he can disagree with Welch on this point, but dismiss it as unimportant.

I generally took the first course early in my patriotic career. I studied *The Politician* thoroughly without finding the famous Welch accusation. Later someone showed me a copy of the original manuscript. Sure enough it said: "[It is] my firm belief that Dwight Eisenhower is a dedicated, conscious agent of the Communist conspiracy *He is!* . . . based on an accumulation of detailed evidence so extensive and so palpable that it seems to me to put this conviction beyond any reasonable doubt." How much more of a Communist could one be? Most Birchers are completely in the dark about this. They were never told that the original version of *The Politician* was cleaned up and toned down before being printed in later editions.

The book gives convincing rationalization for anyone predisposed to believe it on faith and not notice that the information given about Eisenhower's record is grossly unbalanced. There's no attempt to present the pros and cons of the issue. Welch overwhelms his reader with one-sided information, like defensive linemen blitz a vulnerable quarterback.

I find it hard to square *The Politician* with the statement Welch makes time and time again in print and on film, "We do not bear false witness against anybody, about anything." Welch has a similar problem in calling *He was.* former Secretary of State John Foster Dulles a Communist agent. He once reneged on his 1946 observation that Charles de Gaulle is a Communist. But now he apologizes for this lapse on his part of "*not* pointing our finger at a Communist as soon as we should have." After de Gaulle appeared to be moving closer to Moscow in the late 1960s

37

Welch began crowing "I told you so." The Birch Society has a lot of face at stake in seeing America sink into the abyss of collectivism and foreign intrigue they have prophesied.

The basic premise that holds the Society's program together is that the U.S. government is now completely *It is.* under Communist control. As Welch phrases it in the film presentation shown to prospective recruits, ". . . Moscow and Washington are, and for many years have been, but two hands of one body controlled by one brain." He once told me in private, "You understand, of course, that our actual enemy is the U.S. government." *– True.*

At times this leads to some rather amusing mental gymnastics. Whenever the Communists suffer a setback —especially if it comes at the hands of our government —the apparent Communist defeat must in reality be a victory, since decisions made by those who determine U.S. policy are necessarily subservient to Communist plans. Welch calls this tactic "exact reversal."

Take, for example, the Hungarian uprising of 1956. To Welch it was immediately obvious that the Hungarian revolt "had been deliberately planned and precipitated by Moscow's agents" for the purpose of luring out and destroying underground resistance before it became too strong. The war in Vietnam is for the purpose "just to be at war" in order to facilitate fastening a domestic dictatorship upon America. When the Indonesians had a bellyful of Communism and rose up to slay Communists by the tens of thousands, Welch insisted it was caused by the Conspiracy in order to replace one bungling Communist dictator with another. The Israeli-Arab dispute is especially bewildering for many Birchers who believe the

38

Jews have something to do with the Communist conspiracy; they can't figure out why the Russians would want to equip the Arabs to attack the Israelis.) If it weren't so pathetic their frenzied interpretations would make an exciting musical comedy.

Welchian logic has amazed and amused me for some time. It is now being used to quietly change the Birch Society's concept of "the enemy." This new enemy is a super-conspiracy, one that masterminds other conspiracies—including Communism. Welch calls these super-conspirators "The Insiders."

39

3

An Insider Under
Every Bed

The John Birch Society used to joust with only one conspiracy—the international Communist conspiracy. For this they were ridiculed as seeing a Communist under every bed. That joke ought to be revised. Now Welch sees an Insider under every bed.

Welch officially introduced this new radical concept into the Birch philosophy in November, 1966. It appeared in an article entitled "The Truth In Time," which since has been put on film for recruiting meetings. He views the Insider conspiracy as a continuous, secret, historical and dedicated procession of diabolical human beings who are efficiently proceeding to enslave the entire world. Welch believes this conspiratorial chain is 200 years old and is rooted in European secret societies that planned and ignited the French Revolution. The Communist conspiracy, Welch says, evolved from these societies and burst upon the world in 1848 with the publication of Karl Marx's *Communist Manifesto*.

But "the Communist movement is only a tool of the total conspiracy," Welch emphasizes. "As secret as the Communist activities and organizations generally appear, they are part of an open book compared to the secrecy enveloping some higher degree of this diabolic force." Welch says some leaders of this ruling clique are Communists, others are not. In any event, it's so secret that only Robert Welch seems to know about it.

According to "The Truth in Time", the Insiders have used Communists, anarchists, socialists and syndicalists to ferment revolution, subversion, war, famine and terror for the purpose of enslaving the total world population in the 1970s. In America the Insiders have already brought about the Federal Reserve System (conceived by wicked international bankers), the graduated income tax, and the democratic election of United States Senators—all Communist plots to destroy America. The Insiders have been financed principally by tax-exempt foundations which enable the wealthiest Insiders to accumulate billions of tax-free dollars in order to promote their conspiracies.

In the Birch gospel according to Welch, the greatest achievement of the Insiders to date was their instigation of World War I which was "deliberately contrived by power hungry criminal megalomaniacs . . . simply to serve their own purposes." The Insiders also financed and directed Lenin and Trotsky, who were only agents of the Insiders (no doubt hoping to be promoted to Insider-First-Class any day). When these two seized power in

41

Russia, Communism became the palpable Insider front organization.

The next important victory for the Insiders was persuading President Franklin D. Roosevelt to grant diplomatic recognition to Russia in 1933. As Welch says, ". . . this step marked the beginning of the alliance between Washington and Moscow. . . ." Stalin, who Welch says was not necessarily an Insider, also started World War II to align Russia with the West in order to get Lend-Lease aid. Russia's alliance with Hitler at the beginning of the war was just a foil to get the war started, Welch explains. Later, the Insiders had Germany invade Russia so that Stalin would be on the winning side and could manipulate the Western leaders to serve Insider purposes.

With this intricate maneuver accomplished, the Insiders put Operation Exact Reversal into effect. In the name of freedom and independence they launched anticolonialism as a way of swiping small nations from Western empires and annexing them to the Communist world. They started the American foreign aid program—which Welch says was conceived, founded and controlled by Communists—to finance Communist conquests of friendly nations. The United Nations—again conceived, founded and controlled by Communists as an Insider front—was also set up to carry out the Communist global program. In fact, Welch says, "Since early 1945 the most powerful single force in promoting Communism everywhere, and in turning one nation after another over to Communist tyranny . . . has been the help of the United States Government to that end."

The Insider concept is a handy tool for the Birch Society. Birchers have been somewhat handicapped by the libel laws against calling someone a Communist. Actual membership in the Communist Party, Birchers would argue, is a mere technicality that should not prevent Birchers from calling a spade a spade. They are fond of explaining that if something looks like a duck, quacks like a duck and waddles like a duck, chances are it is a duck. Likewise, if someone acts like a Communist and talks like a Communist, then he must actually be one. Although "Communist" is a dirty word, Birchers figure they can call people "Insiders" without creating a fuss. The trouble is that except for themselves no one knows what an Insider is.

The Insider concept pleases the general membership in another way, too. One of Welch's main problems has been that some Birchers pressure him to "tell it like it is" and expose Communism as a Jewish plot. The Insider conspiracy serves as a convenient sop to these people. They use "Insider" as a synonym for the "Zionists" they preach are the root of all the world's problems.

Welch has not cleared up these useful misunderstandings by naming the contemporary Insiders. He has said that the inner sanctum once included Lenin, Colonel Edward House (President Wilson's influential adviser), Sidney Hillman and Nehru. But this is a safe concession on his part—they're all dead and can't fight back.

This who-are-they. question presents problems for Birch field staff members who have to show the Insider film presentation. Most of them just mention the Council on Foreign Relations, the Bilderbergers, "big money interests" (sometimes a code name for Jews) or some other liberal organizations they can burden with the onus of subversion.

The only name of a living American I've actually heard high ranking Birch professionals mention as an Insider is William F. Buckley, Jr., who many Americans would consider the most articulate and responsible right-winger in the nation. Practically everyone in the Society assumes that New York's Governor Nelson Rockefeller is an Insider.

Reaction to the new and fantastic Insider concept among rank and file Birchers has been extremely apathetic, all things considered. There is one exception I know personally: a Catholic priest who joined the Society before he knew what it was all about was appalled when he finally saw a film presentation about the Insiders. His chapter leader, a fanatical Catholic traditionalist, sent the following comments to Birch headquarters:

"Rev. ——— who attended his first meeting in February, has since had 'second thoughts' about joining The John Birch Society. He disagrees with Mr. Welch on his stand on the 'INSIDERS' and I have urged Father ——— to write Belmont about this problem. While we were, at first, delighted at having a Catholic priest and former pastor join our group, we since have found Father ——— to be the greatest threat to our chapter since we began with the Society. If Father ——— were to remain with our group, rather than expressing the wish to resign, I would have considered him a 'plant.'"

The good priest's overt reaction to the Insider concept was the first and only time I witnessed anyone openly question some of the fantastic generalizations Welch makes about Communism and its influence on America. As a coordinator for the John Birch Society it never ceased to amaze me with what aplomb Americans accept whatever incredible pronouncements are presented on film with any sort of pretense of research and scholarship.

4

Every Night at the Movies

My main irresponsibility as a professional patriot for the Birch Society was to hold presentation meetings for prospective members. While the American public was enjoying Wednesday and Friday nights at the movies on televison, I was enduring every night at the movies at Birch meetings.

Presentation meetings were arranged at the homes of Birch members on a fairly regular schedule which took me on a constant tour of the southern half of Florida. Birchers were exhorted to proceed with recruiting efforts on a carefully worked-out basis. Whenever a Bircher observed anyone complaining about the trend of things in general, he was to pounce upon the unfortunate individual and test his attitude on such things as taxation, Vietnam, civil rights and other contemporary irritations and disorders. If probing produced sufficient discontent to be exploited, the next step was to bring Birchism into the conversation and persuade the prospect to purchase a *Blue Book* for one dollar.

Every prospect was supposed to have read the *Blue Book* before he was brought to a presentation meeting to be signed up as a bona fide Bircher. This seldom worked according to plan. Usually, the people who showed up at presentations were totally ignorant of what the Society was all about and without the slightest intention of joining such a nutty organization.

Most Birchers' idea of recruiting new members approximated shanghaiing reluctant relatives, neighbors or tourists; driving them to the meeting in secrecy; and dumping them onto my lap with a smug attitude of: "Well, I got 'em here pal. Now you give them the works and sign 'em up." On occasion, people were transported to our movies without the slightest notion that they were attending a Birch meeting. This would cause a bit of a stir when I got around to introducing myself.

Entire chapters of insecure Birchers sometimes pursued recruiting as a collective project, seeking relative safety in numbers. Usually they preferred to canvass neighborhoods on the other side of town where no one would know them. At times they formed teams of two and went door-to-door asking startled occupants if they knew anything about the John Birch Society. If the door was slammed in their face it was obvious the people already knew too much about the Society. If their introduction was met with a blank expression, they had a live prospect on their hands.

Other chapters preferred to do their soliciting over the

47

telephone, figuring that a slammed receiver in the ear is a lot less humiliating than a slammed door in the face. More timid Birchers were encouraged to organize direct mail campaigns of selected pamphlets with return addresses of impersonal post office box numbers to which interested prospects could respond.

Many Birch prospects came from lists of people who wrote to the national headquarters in Massachusetts for information on how to go about finding a genuine Bircher in their locality. These leads were then filtered back to the local area of origin and active Birch members were assigned to make contact, begin indoctrination and bring the prospect to a presentation meeting.

On presentation night in any Florida locality I would show up in my Volkswagen bus (even though foreign cars were frowned upon by Birchers) at exactly 7:30 P.M. and begin to carry in my retinue of equipment and merchandise: 16 mm. Bell & Howell Filmomatic Sound Projector, heavy-duty movie screen, several large reels of film, and multi-copies of six or seven basic Birch books to be displayed for sale. Next came the diplomatic chore of convincing my hostess to permit me to rearrange her living room for better seating capacity. While the lady fretted over each arriving guest, I went about my business of threading my projector, setting up the screen, appropriating tables for book displays and generally keeping busy in order to avoid, as much as possible, the tiresome small talk of early arrivals.

Usually, the host chapter would absolutely count on twenty to twenty-five "definitely-committed" prospects to show up for the presentation. By movie time five or six people would have called with outlandish last-minute

48

excuses. When we finally got down to business (half an hour later to accommodate the late-arrivals who were "absolutely coming for sure," but never showed up), there were hardly ever more than five or six faithfuls on hand for the final pitch.

Various kinds of people come to Birch presentations. The largest number are reluctant guests dragged to the meeting by enthusiastic Birch relatives. Closely allied with them are business associates or close acquaintances who feel indebted to courteously indulge a good friend's eccentricity. They dutifully and patiently put in their time, and then leave as quickly as they can politely run out on the group afterwards. When the movie is over they pump your hand with vigor, smile firmly with finality and murmur some triviality that speeds them on their way—such as, "Well, thank you so very much. I really enjoyed your movies." It is inconceivable that anyone could sit through movies filled with Red atrocities and dire warnings that the Communist conspiracy is about to get you and actually enjoy the evening.

The second largest group of Birch movie fans are curiosity-seekers who derive pleasure savoring every juicy morsel of right-wing propaganda. They generally contribute total participation to the meeting, asking every conceivable question and giving rapt attention when the books are being sold. Of course, these funsters have no intention of joining the Society, but they get satisfaction from leading anxious members on a merry chase trying to persuade them to take that final plunge into extremism.

In Florida many of the people in the last category are tourists indulging themselves in a fling into radicalism

49

far away from home. The tourists wouldn't be caught dead at a Birch meeting up North.

The biggest fun group of all are the college fraternity pledges who are obliged to get a Birch application blank as part of "hell week" activities. They go to great lengths to prove their sincerity in order to wheedle invitations to presentations from unsuspecting Birchers. I could always spot the frat boys at intermission; they invariably buy up all the "Impeach Earl Warren" bumper strips to decorate their dormitory rooms. I thoroughly enjoyed their presence because it is easy to get their dander up by flinging a few outrageous insults at left-wing professors and lazy Hippies. One devoted freshman radical got so riled that he challenged me to a duel.

The most persistent and irritating spectators at Birch presentations are the fundamentalist religious fanatics who don't come to learn, but to convert everyone in sight into a "born again" Christian. Usually their missionary zeal drives them into a frenzied and most un-Christian tirade against The National Council of Churches, which they regard as a Communist front organization. When one or two of these apostles show up it's a fight to the finish to determine whether everyone in the room goes Birch, or to a nearby creek to be baptized.

The most pathetic group of prospects for the Birch Society consists of retired senior citizens who crave companionship under any conditions and weirdos who are attracted to anything off the beaten track. The old people find it difficult to stay awake through two hours of film, and the crackpots make fools out of themselves before anyone can even get them signed up.

Once I gave an afternoon presentation to a small,

smug group of prudish old ladies who all fell asleep in the Victorian sitting room before I could get the second reel of film threaded through the projector. I had questioned the usefulness of giving a presentation to these ladies since it was obvious they had not retired to Florida to live, but to die. When my host assured me they still had enough strength left in them to scratch out a few letters to newspaper editors about impeaching Earl Warren, I carried on with the presentation.

The only spark that was left was ignited during the question-and-answer period when one sober-looking spinster came out of her coma long enough to ask, "Young man, how do you stand on light beer and wine?" I chuckled happily, heartened by her effort, and replied without thinking, "I'm all for 'em. Could use a short snort right now!" It was a highly unsatisfactory answer. She had been an officer of the Women's Christian Temperance Union.

At the end of the ordeal they all resurrected themselves and shuffled drowsily from the room. The last of the ladies turned at the door, yawned, pressed something into my hand and mumbled, "I'm not much on politics, sonny. But here's a donation for your trouble."

With the weird people who were often on hand, presentation meetings could have been quite eventful. Unfortunately, however, there was a divine injunctive from Belmont that stubbornly insisted that we show their ungodly movies. My job at a presentation, then, was mainly that of official greeter, peace and order keeper, film introducer, Birch book purveyor and sales closer.

I probably was the only Birch coordinator in the country who totally "winged it" at every meeting. I was fond of

51

explaining over and over to nervous hosts that my approach was always custom tailored to fit the unique characteristics of each group of prospective patriots. What I didn't tell them was that every living room full of prospects was damn well the same and that I varied my sales pitch because it was my only possible way to keep from going stark raving mad. I never knew what I was going to say before I arrived at that dreadful moment when I finally had to face the kooky little crowd and turn on some sort of half-way convincing performance. When I wasn't up to it, my presentations exhibited an appalling lack of serious preparation. But mostly I lucked out and things fell into place well.

As my prospects settled in for a long evening's nap, my opening comments usually went something like this:

"I want to thank you folks for showing up tonight to hear the John Birch story. It takes a lot of courage for you to be here in the first place after all the propaganda you've heard about us being fascists, hate-mongers, racists, anti-Semites and just plain kooks. Just being here means you've got an open mind and we sincerely thank you for waiting to hear our side of the story before you make up your own mind.

"I'm not going to say much at this point. You're going to be seeing two hours of film and we want to leave you plenty of time to ask questions at the end of the evening. Be sure to ask every embarrassing question you can think of. We know you've got tough questions on your mind. Let's get them all out in the open so we can get to the heart of your hesitation. We've got all the confidence in the world we can clear up your qualms and absolutely convince you that the John Birch Society is the greatest, most idealistic organization in America, composed of the finest, most religious, most dedicated people you'll ever find anywhere.

52

"Before I turn off the lights and turn on my projector, I want you to know a little bit about Robert Welch, the founder of the John Birch Society. For the next two hours he's going to be talking to each of you—man to man—about the tremendous problems our great nation faces, the cause of all these great problems and the programs and projects the John Birch Society proposes as a solution.

"You've all heard about Robert Welch, I'm sure. He's been called every name in the book by practically everybody—TV, radio, newspapers and Washington. As you know, he's a racist, a bigot, a hater, a Nazi . . . he's everything evil and treacherous. That's what you've been led to believe by the press and by all the enemies of our great nation.

"But I'm not going to counter all this garbage with my opinions—or anybody else's opinions about Robert Welch. I'm going to let the facts speak for themselves.

"Robert Welch was born . . . ancestors helped settle America . . . read all the volumes of Ridpath's *History of the World* by the age of seven . . . led his class at Annapolis . . . led class at Harvard Law School . . . unlike everyone else from Harvard, Welch did not turn left after graduation . . . went into the family candy business . . . was a leader in National Chamber of Commerce. . . .

"At this point Robert Welch realized something was drastically wrong with America. He saw nation after nation being lost to the Communists. Disastrous mistakes were being made in foreign affairs. Our State Department never seemed to do anything right. Robert Welch wondered why.

"As a businessman, Robert Welch knew the solid strength of the amazing American free enterprise system. He knew what made it work. He knew this system was responsible for our nation's fantastic wealth, know-how and high standard of living—the highest standard of living the world has ever seen. The free-enterprise system made America great, not the

53

bureaucrats in Washington who live off your tax money, and not the atheistic, left-wing beatnik professors who never produced a single thing in their lives besides idle talk, unworkable theories and discontent among our confused and pampered youth.

"Robert Welch saw the gradual erosion of the free enterprise system in America by some alien, socialistic, welfare schemes imported from England. He began to do some serious thinking about this, serious thinking that we all should do. He severed all his business ties, travelled around the world to talk to leaders like Chiang Kai-shek and studied Communism extensively. Finally he had the answers to all the terrible questions. Yes, there was a conspiracy—a deep-rooted conspiracy—a Communist conspiracy aimed at conquering the world.

"Next Mr. Welch went to work to come up with a practical way to stop this conspiracy, a way to preserve our wonderful system which we inherited from unselfish ancestors who gave their blood to see that we had freedom.

"The three reels of film you are about to see will tell you how we got into the mess we're in today, the horrifying mess that makes you willing to come here tonight despite all you've heard about the Birch Society. In this film Robert Welch will also tell you what he aims to do about this mess, and how you can help save America for your children and your children's children by joining the John Birch Society.

"Well, I've already talked too much. Robert Welch tells it much better than I. Please make yourself comfortable while I start the projector."

Then came the great letdown, at least for me. Two hours of the flickering father image of the little old man. Two hours of Robert Welch sputtering endlessly in his monotone, machine gun delivery. Two hours of some of the most incredible perversions of history imaginable.

The total lack of reaction to the story Robert Welch tells never ceased to amaze me.

There were four film presentations available from the Society, all of which I could practically recite by heart. *A Look At the Score,* the original and most widely used presentation, was made in 1960 and is an amateurish, verbatim recitation of most of Welch's *Blue Book.* The concluding third reel begins with a fluttering 5–4–3–2–1 countdown followed by Welch's screen-filling, fatherly face saying, "My friends of the American Republic. . . ." Welch then says he will try in the last 27 minutes to tell a story that usually takes two days (I can believe it). He remembers how the Society was founded, why it is under attack, some of the Congressmen who endorse Birch members as friends but stop short of endorsing the Society, why the membership is secret, and how you can find out all about the Society (he recommends buying a five dollar introductory packet). Welch also outlines the objectives of the Society: less government, more individual responsibility and a better world. "It is better to light one candle than to curse the darkness," he says. And, as a matter of fact, you can purchase a whole set of books called "One Dozen Candles" for ten dollars. "The Communists don't like it," Welch says. "They can't stand the truth."

This is Welch's pet presentation and he long resisted the membership's insistent demands that something more professional be worked up that would at least use charts and maps to relieve the tedium of one and a half uninterrupted hours of Robert Welch. Finally, a slick, expensive movie was made. This one was crammed with gorgeous art work and various shots of the home office in

55

Belmont showing the dedicated staff working their heads
off to preserve our Republic and bring Communism to a
screeching halt. There were also glorious testimonials
given by a Congressman, several "average" housewives, a
mechanic, a businessman, a doctor, a minister, a priest
and a Negro woman who seemed somewhat peeved about
her role. There was somebody there for everybody. Supposedly, even a Jewish rabbi was lined up for testimony,
but was mysteriously transferred to Israel before he
could go before the Birch cameras. The movie was a
great hit with the membership who enjoyed watching the
antics of the busy-bee staff in Belmont and all the humming machines their dues money had paid for. The only
problem was that while the Society was portrayed in a
most favorable manner, there was very little material
that provided motivation to join.

When recruitment dwindled to nothing, Welch filmed
another mundane fireside chat, entitled *A Touch of Sanity*. This film explained thoroughly what was wrong with
America and how Welch proposed to get us all out of this
"vast insane asylum which was being run by the worst
inmates."

When the attraction of this film wore off, Welch again
went before the cameras to give Presentation Film Number Four, consisting of the most radical of his concepts
about the Insiders. This one made even some of our
staunchest supporters go into hiding when they were
asked to bring their friends to see it.

A special directive concerning this film was sent to all
field men by Tom Hill, director of Birch field activities.
He said there have been "numerous complaints on the
new film, primarily as to its depth. And these comments

have come not only from weak members but from several of my best Section Leaders. They say the film is just too much for a nonmember. Unfortunately, I understand what they really are saying: it is too deep for many members as well."

The memorandum went on to emphasize that field men should stick to their guns in the face of these complaints and not deviate one inch. Hill admitted that "we have a job to do in persuading our members to look at Film Number Four in its proper perspective." The understatement of the year.

I managed to sidestep this directive for a few weeks by alternating the other presentations or mixing up several reels from each of the presentations for a tossed salad effect. But Belmont eventually made it clear that variety wasn't the spice of life and I had better book the Insider film for a long run.

The worst part of my coordinator's job was sitting through a Birch film every night and looking like I was enjoying every minute of it. Unfortunately, the only bright place in the room was right next to my projector where I was brilliantly conspicuous during the entire performance. The rest of the old Birch hands were either lucky or devious. They found various nooks and crannies where they could secretly snooze, or retreated into the kitchen on the pretense of slaving over the inevitable cookies and coffee served after the second reel.

The trick for coordinators was to put yourself in the right frame of mind, like a football player psyching himself for the big game. But this seldom worked for me since it obviously wasn't a very big game I was playing. The only ploy that succeeded was to put on a phony face and think of something far removed from Birchism—something pleasant, like how to get home early, or the big tankard of beer that awaited me when I got there.

Another distraction that I enjoyed immensely was to study each prospect carefully and figure out what they might be thinking. Most of the time I concluded that they were thinking the same thoughts I was: how to get home early for that big tankard of beer.

Occasionally, when hot film flashes of Robert Welch momentarily lit up the room like a Roman candle, I could catch one of our prospects taking a cat nap. That's when I tested my ESP to see what havoc I could wreak. Riveting my unblinking eyes on their slumbering hulk, I would bore into their subconscious like a laser beam and think over and over, "Wake up, Chicken Little. We're all in this together." If my target as much as twitched, which he rarely did, I would fire round two of my psychological barrage. "You have to go to the bathroom, booby. You have to go to the bathroom." If that didn't work, and it never did, I would turn my attention to the telephone and try, to brainwash it into ringing with a bomb threat that would necessitate clearing the room at once. That never worked either.

Once, however, we heard a car door slam violently in front of the house and then a car peel rubber all the way down the street. When I went outside to have a look around, I found the front door of my VW bus wide open and a maze of wires sticking out of a heap of rubble on the floor. My immediate conclusion was that it was a huge bomb and I got away from there full speed ahead. After my courage returned, my friends watched as I tiptoed back with a flashlight and discovered that someone had pulled the radio out of my dashboard and left behind all the loose wires and a floor full of my own glove compartment junk. It was most embarrassing.

The best I could normally hope for was that a late arrival would shatter the gloom by ringing the doorbell. Then at least I could shout happily, "Sorry folks, I think it's another raid!"

Once I was presented with the perfect predicament to enliven a meeting: relatives unexpectedly dropped in on some of our most secretive members just as I was lurching into my sales pitch for *Blue Books* and bumper strips. "Well, what's this, a Communist cell meeting?" the innocent interlopers asked humorously. "Oh, no," I answered gleefully, "it's a John Birch cell meeting. Come on in and conspire with us." As the hosts recoiled in horror, the hilarity disappeared immediately. Luckily, I remembered my infatuation with those lovely little weekly Birch paychecks quickly enough to smooth over the whole ugly situation.

The most delicate fix to be in was to have to lecture guests on issues that they were much more intimately associated with than I. This most often occurred when promoting our Vietnam project with Vietnam veterans in the audience. Suggesting to them that the war in Vietnam was just a sham battle concocted by Washington and Moscow to drain our resources of men and money for the Communist conspiracy wasn't the safest thing in the world. I was always pleased to be tipped off in advance when there were GI's with us so I could call on them to tell us what it was like at the front. I would interrupt to inject little gems of patriotism, such as "Yes sir, folks, we back our boys all the way." The war issue

59

was hell for Birch coordinators with soldiers around. It was especially sensitive for me since I had never been closer to the army than applying for deferments at the registrar's office in college.

The most unexpected protest I ever had to contend with was a policeman who questioned the validity of our successful slogan "Support Your Local Police." I had never had any problems with this highly popular campaign before. It seemed as sure as sponsoring the school safety patrol program, the girl scouts or bingo for charity. When the protestor identified himself as a member of the Dade County police force in Miami, I asked if he thought there was a better way we could go about getting the public behind the local men in blue. "Hell no!" he replied with an explosion. "The police department is as crooked as the tailpipe on a Cadillac. You shouldn't support it at all." Somehow I never quite anticipated a development like that and it thoroughly ruined my evening's work. I almost forgot to sell my books that night.

As much as I hated the movies we were compelled to show, my greatest fear as a coordinator was that some night my projector would break down before a houseful of people and I would be forced to ad lib the whole show. I could recite the film presentation by heart, to be sure, but then that would be rather nonsensical coming from me directly in person rather than Our Father Robert Welch on celluloid.

I took precautions against this by carrying every conceivable spare part in the pocket of the expensive leather cover that accompanied the projector. Just the same, the mere thought of such a spectacle sent chills up my spine and sweat into my palms. The closest I ever came to a machinery breakdown was the night that the take-up reel arm suddenly stopped taking up. My razor-sharp mechanical mind found an instantaneous, though excruciatingly painful, solution. I thrust my finger into the dawdling reel and twirled the heavy thing around by hand for a full hour before the crisis had passed and the Insiders had been thoroughly brought out into the open.

Between reels I had the job of selling Birch books, pamphlets and other items which earned me a hefty 40 per cent commission. The standard fare consisted of copies of the *Blue Book, The Politician* and a baker's dozen boxed series of 13 books called "One Dozen Candles." Welch referred to the books in this series as "suppressed books" and coordinators pitch them as hot anti-Communist items that give the real inside story on Communism in America. Today, believe it or not, the set has been revised and it is called Ten Neon Torches, or TNT. Imagine trying to keep a straight face while selling something by that name.

The real work began when the film was finally over and it was time to try to sign somebody up for the duration of the cold war. First there was a question and answer period with members planted to ask the right questions in case the prospects didn't. The most important thing here was to convince everyone that the only possible way they could fight Communism was to join the Society and actively work with a nationally coordinated body of dedicated zealots on specifically selected projects. In winding up the presentation I would go to great lengths to point out that it was difficult to get into the Birch Society since we only admitted the finest men and women in the world. Then I indicated they had all been sized up as worthy for this honor and could join as soon as they felt ready. "There's no hurry. No pressure. Read all our material. Think it over carefully, if you like." Then we closed the meeting with a prayer and teams of Birch members took individual prospects aside and cajoled, begged, twisted arms and did everything conceivable to sign up anybody who could breathe, hate Communists with every heartbeat and write letters to Congressmen and editors by the score.

Almost every prospect would dodge, dart, rationalize and melt away as fast as possible without signing any papers or committing themselves to any more meetings. I felt truly sorry for our members. When practically everybody had left, we would make our only scores for the evening. The man or woman who joined the Society would usually wait until the very end and then slither up and sign an application blank with obvious haste. The applicants, with very few exceptions, would be people who had not asked any questions, had not shown the slightest interest throughout the presentation, and would, by all appearances, seem to be the least likely to join a radical organization.

In general, Birchers are the "least likely" people in the world. Robert Welch is the least likely looking leader of radicals. I was the least likely type to be the center of local storms of controversy. Our members were the least likely people imaginable to provide a constant—though pathetic—supply of unintentional humor.

5

Coming Through the Wry

If one were to list the most interesting jobs in the world, coordinator for the John Birch Society would have to be placed near the top. Not only does the work offer every pitfall imaginable, but the people you work with are capable of doing practically anything, except what you would normally expect.

You can't even be sure how your best members will react when you meet them in public. Due to their great anxiety about revealing their Birchism to friends and relatives, they would just as soon snub you on the street as make an introduction that could reveal that they're a bit kooky. If being a Birch coordinator affects other Birchers that way, you can imagine what it is like to meet or work with non-Birchers who know no more about the JBS than what they read in the newspapers.

It's an experience just to drive around and watch people react to right-wing bumper strips that Birchers proudly display—bumper strips that demand such things as: "Impeach Earl Warren"; "Register Communists, Not Firearms"; "Save Our Republic—Join the John Birch Society." Even "Support Your Local Police" can garner some mean stares—especially when you're nervously driving through a ghetto on a Friday or Saturday night. "Repeal the Income Tax" attracts sympathy, a chuckle and then the comment which I learned to lip read at a great distance, "What are you, some kind of a nut?" Get the US Out of the UN" earns blank looks of bewilderment from all motorists, as if they never heard of either the UN or the U.S. Many people read it as *get the us out of the un,* which, of course, can be slightly puzzling to a member of the silent majority.

But, as I found out, the study of people is always a two-way street. I was once invited to the University of Miami in Florida to lecture to a sociology class about the John Birch Society. Halfway through the question and answer period it suddenly dawned on me that they weren't interested in our organization at all. I, Gerald Schomp, a specimen of right-wing extremism, was the topic of the day to be carefully analyzed, classified, labelled and filed away for future reference. I think it was the first time I actually realized I was a curiosity—one of the very nuts and kooks I so much enjoyed telling my wife about at the end of a long day of work.

Nevertheless, curiosity often worked in my favor. Whenever I spoke at a civic club luncheon, a new attendance record was invariably set. When it was time for my introduction I could read the same haunting question in

64

every pair of eyes that momentarily looked up from the jello, "Hmmmm, what have we here today for our amusement?" It was like a den of lions toying with a fresh piece of meat.

My very first experience as a sideshow performer especially unnerved me. When I took my place at the head table before unloading my Birch barrage at the Sertoma Club in St. Petersburg, I discovered they had a news photographer on hand to snap close-up pictures of me every time I lifted my fork to eat a lamb chop. (I was ridiculed in the newspaper for being so nervous that I hardly touched my lunch.) When I stood up to speak (weaker than usual since I had no nourishment) the photographer popped up right in front of me and blocked my view of the very quiet audience. I finally got rid of the shutterbug by opening my talk with this comment: "If you've been having trouble getting coverage from the press, I suggest you invite the John Birch Society to lunch every week." Later, one of the club officials called for the organization of a new society for the preservation of wooden toilet seats; he called it "The Birch John Society." I used to get particularly peeved at the civic clubs when I noticed each group seemed to "accidentally" misspell my name the same way on the customary certificate of appreciation which is given to each speaker. They usually spelled it "Gerald H. Chump."

Tableside chatter was perhaps the most interesting aspect of my time spent as a public clown for civic club luncheons. The members—whether Moose, Lions, Sertomaons, Eagles, Kiwanians, Jaycees, Rotarians, Optimists, Pessimists, or what have you—were always most eager to find out what sort of a chap I was. At first they

65

would probe a bit by taking a few unkind cuts at what they usually termed "race-mixin' niggers" and suggested that maybe the KKK was just looking out for everyone's best interests after all. When I made it as clear as possible that I felt Negroes were entitled to the same rights as everyone else, the civic-minded folks suddenly would be at a loss for words until someone thought to try a different track.

At this point I got my own cheap thrills by baiting every businessman around me into condemning federal give-away programs as a surefire socialistic road to pure totalitarianism. They would fall all over themselves damning Washington, bureaucrats, Yankees, tax collectors, Congress, and Walter Cronkite. "We've got to fight back . . . enough is enough . . . turn the rascals out . . . ," they would bleat. Then I would extract *my* pound of flesh by humbly suggesting that perhaps *they* ought to go to work in *their* area and convince *their* own Congressman to reject all federal aid for *their* district in order to set an example of hometown, do-it-yourself pride for the rest of the nation to follow.

It was fascinating to watch them wallow in this predicament and slip out clumsily with the usual rationalizations: "Well, now . . . really, you know . . . it's actually our money to begin with . . . we have to get our fair share . . . if we don't somebody else will . . . we need the money right now in this area . . . folks around here are up to their ears in taxes . . . we need the help in order to get things going . . . the change will have to come from the top . . . after all, things are very complex today and more centralization is necessary . . . blah, blah, blah."

66

College appearances were always the most exciting episodes in my work. At one Catholic college, for instance, I drew the largest crowd they had ever had—no mean feat since the controversial Bishop James Pike had been there two weeks earlier.

As a right-winger in an age when most teenagers are very liberal, the only way I could win any friends at these events was to topple some hypersensitive, crusty old prof who couldn't contain himself in my presence. At this Catholic School I was troubled with one particular professor who kept interrupting my talk with crude remarks, such as "You fascists are all alike. . . . Put a sheet over him and he'd sound like any other bigot." When he loudly proclaimed, "You're full of hot air," I pointed dramatically to the door and demanded, "If you don't like it, I suggest you go outside and get some fresh air." The students applauded wildly and the professor was properly put down for the rest of the evening.

My glory lasted no more than a scant five minutes. When a sweet little Negro coed stood up bravely to challenge the Birch contention that the Communist conspiracy was controlling the Negro civil rights movement, there wasn't anything I could have said to shift the balance of power back my way.

Whenever I spoke at a college that had a chapter of Students for a Democratic Society, I knew I was in for an especially lively engagement. Usually, as I walked into the student union building I could expect to be met by a bunch of bedraggled student replicas of Fidel Castro. They could always be counted upon to shout some sweet welcome. For example, "The Nazi from the Birch Gestapo is here. Let's kill him." At this crucial moment, if I was lucky, a more respectable student type would come to my rescue and apologize halfheartedly for the extra-warm, unofficial reception. "It's nothing," I would quietly blubber in relief. "Boys will be boys."

Occasionally I had the opportunity to escort profes-sional American Opinion lecturers while they were in the area for speaking engagements. One of these, Mrs. Julia Brown, a Negro who had spent nine years as an FBI undercover informer in the Communist Party, was one of the most delightful, unpredictable and personable people I've ever met. When I picked her up at the airport we got off to a bad start. I tried to persuade her to sit in the middle seat of my VW station wagon for her own com-fort. She set her jaw firm, her eyes bulged like flame-throwers and she told me, "I'm not going to the back of anybody's bus for anything."

Before long, however, she cooled off and we got along fabulously for the next four days of her lecture series. She also did a number of radio interviews—each of them a gem of an experience. A scrawny Miami radio personal-ity, Larry King, stoked up her fire when he called Robert Welch a "fink." Julia nearly scared him out of his sandals when she shot back, "And you're a double fink!" When King ended the program by announcing the time had run out, Julia answered him threateningly: "It's a good thing! I was just about to come over the table after you!"

When another commentator needled her about Ne-groes rioting in the streets, Julia stopped him cold with her summary dismissal, "It's just the black trash being led by the white trash." She wrapped up another inter-view abruptly by asking over the air, "May I go to the bathroom now, please?" On still another station, Julia caused the telephones to ring off the hook when she mistakenly said that Senator Edward Brooke was not the first Negro elected to major office in Massachusetts. "Governor Endicott Peabody is a Negro, you know." This came as a surprise to many people who didn't know—especially Governor Peabody.

Some of our members—and others who were not members but hung around on the fringe of Society activities—had some weird theories about the cause of all the world's problems. As if the Insiders weren't enough, one man was sure he had located the center of the *real* conspiracy in Argentina. He had actually seen the conspirators—Germans in World War II uniforms who flew out of their underground headquarters in flying saucers.

A top radio announcer in St. Petersburg had an almost equally bizarre idea about Communism. In his opinion there was only one group who could possibly save this country from Communism—the Mafia! He reasoned that our own domestic criminals were so well organized that they could and would knock the bejabbers out of Communist international gangsters.

A man who attended one of my presentations at Pompano Beach, Florida (a leader in his church who appeared to be quite intelligent—otherwise)—was convinced that Outsiders (not Insiders) from the planet Pluto were causing all our distress. It seems our position in the heavens relative to Pluto creates "influence cycles" which periodically incite men to war and revolution. He concluded that men do not have free will and therefore nothing can be done to improve international relations.

Another man—a genius who is a multi-millionaire inventor—invited me to his luxurious winter home in the

69

Florida Keys to tell me that he had stumbled upon the Communist method of financing subversive activities. He had just been cheated out of one of his trust funds and was sure this was happening all over. He wanted me to put a round-the-clock watch on some of his former business associates who had retired to Naples, a Florida resort town. One of the Society's coordinators in a different state considered this information extremely valuable and wanted us to write a book about it.

On another occasion I came close to getting hurt by a man with a monkey on his back—a real monkey that damn near sank his razor sharp teeth into me. This man had written to the Society for assistance in his legal struggle with the Federal government. After driving 50 miles to get to his small place east of Tampa, I found his trailer lot posted with "No Trespassing—Violators Will Be Shot" signs. As if to emphasize this point, his 11-year-old son was on the front steps cleaning a wicked-looking musket which his father must have saved from a stint in the Confederate Army. I slipped out of my VW gingerly, so as not to needlessly startle anyone.

"Is your father home?" I cooed gently.

"What's it to you?" he asked without looking up.

"He wrote a letter to me and asked me to come and see him," I replied.

"Pa can't write none," he retorted.

"Well, then somebody wrote to me for him," I said. "Is he home and can I see him?"

The boy disappeared into the trailer and his father appeared a moment later. He was a giant of a man with a huge hairy stomach that tumbled over his belt like a waterfall. His head was bald, but his face was bristling with a heavy growth of red brush. On his shoulder was a small monkey that had already begun to scold me.

"Son says you want to see me," he ventured.

"Yes, sir, I'm from the John Birch Society. You wrote and said you had something important for us."

"Oh, yeah. Been spectin' you for some time. Come on in."

Since it was definitely an order, I entered his trailer pronto, but with all conceivable misgivings. There I met his wife, a frail and humbled woman, who I immediately felt immensely sorry for. When we got down to business I had a terrible time with the monkey. He screamed hysterically and nipped at me viciously every time I tried to talk.

All the giant could say was, "Don't pay him no mind. He does it all the time." Small comfort for me as I cowered against the wall. "Picked the chimp up for free from a carnival man not long ago," he explained. "He was going to destroy the monkey 'cause he was so mean. Gave him to me right off when I asked."

"A real bargain," I agreed.

"Haven't had much trouble with him myself," he boasted. Doesn't turn on his own kind, I thought to myself.

The giant's problem was that the government had cut off his Social Security payments when local authorities discovered he was working a sneak job as a caretaker at night. Now he was "fixin'" to sue the government for four million dollars and was advertising for bidders to finance his suit and share in his bonanza. He wondered if the Birch Society would like to buy a piece of his legal defense fund. I advised him that such a thing would be impossible, but that I could supply him with the name and address of someone in Tampa who just might be able to help him. I gladly gave the giant the name of a lawyer in Tampa who I had been trying to get even with for some time.

When the giant told me that the neighbors were giving him trouble, the school authorities were down on him for not sending his boy to school and the trailer park owner was trying to evict him, I willingly donated some of my own money to the defense fund. Anything to get out of there.

I finally made it back to my car, but not without strong encouragement to shake hands with the screaming monkey which promptly nipped me on the knuckle.

Sometimes the kooks are even more dangerous. In 1965 an electronics wizard was actually making bombing runs from an airplane over Miami. The bomber, a 30-year-old bachelor with an I.Q. of 150, was finally arrested after his fifth mission. Using a slide rule and complicated navigational instruments, he would take off at night in a rented plane and drop homemade, gasoline-filled gallon jugs on the homes of Negroes and Jews. He told police that "secret voices" directed him "to scare the Communists who are instigating riots."

These episodes didn't especially interest me until after the bomber had been grounded by the police and the Miami *Herald* had run a front-page story headlined: "Sky Bomber Suspect A John Birch Member?" Few people noticed that this was a question, not a statement of fact.

As the story unfolded, I found that an unemployed former manager of a small aviation business had told the police that two years earlier he had seen what appeared to be a Birch membership card among the bomber's personal effects. With Birchers going up in flames of indignation all over southern Florida, I called our Belmont headquarters and confirmed that the bomber had never been a member of the Birch Society. Later, after questioning Birchers in the vicinity of the bomber's home, I discovered that he *had* been invited to join the Society at a presentation meeting.

I dictated a statement to the *Herald* over the telephone disassociating the Society from the bomber—a statement which they buried on the bottom of page six of the fourth section right next to the obituaries. Perhaps this was symbolic of the fact that our public relations image had been fatally injured a long time before.

Months later the bomber wrote me a letter from his jail cell offering to help the Society if we wanted to sue the *Herald* for libel. He humbly said it was a defamation of our character to claim that he was a Bircher. As it turned out, he had not joined the Society because he knew that he would soon be in trouble with the police for his night flying and did not want to involve us. This was one prospect I'm glad we lost.

In another bombing case in 1962, an active Society member was arrested in one of the most sensational stories in Miami's history. The member was accused of discharging deadly explosives at the home of the editor of the Miami *Herald*. It never became known that he was a member of a Hialeah chapter of the John Birch Society. He was quietly dropped from the rolls when the bombing story hit the headlines. Later, when the case was dismissed in court, the man was not invited back into the Society. Ironically, the leader of that chapter later became a policeman.

In still another novel Miami crime case, a sergeant in the Dade County Sheriff's Office was indicted on three counts of grand larceny, one of petty larceny, one of burglary and one in connection with prostitution. He was eventually acquitted of all charges. I had signed this man up for the Society myself and had considered it quite a feather in my cap. Actually, it was suspiciously easy.

The sergeant called me long distance, asked me to come to his office at police headquarters and requested a membership application blank as soon as I showed up. I thought he was kidding at first and I laughed up a storm. But he soon made it clear he was serious and signed the application in the presence of his boss and several secretaries. When I asked for help in determining whether one of our members was in the Ku Klux Klan, he gave me a complete list of Klan members in two counties. Then he asked for my help in return.

The Sheriff's Office and Dade County's Metropolitan Government with the help of the Miami *Herald* had been fighting a vicious struggle for survival for some time. The sergeant wanted the Birch Society to help discredit Miami's Metro government so that the voters would eliminate the system in a full referendum. Though subsequently cleared of charges, the referendum movement flopped when the sheriff and some of his men were indicted by a grand jury. The Miami *Herald* could have ruined us once and for all if they had known we were even loosely associated with the sheriff's office fiasco.

Miami has been a constant problem for the Society

almost from the beginning. When we opened an American Opinion Book Store there in 1966, we immediately began having serious differences with the manager who was also the owner of the property and a Birch chapter leader. Unauthorized literature was stocked and prominently displayed against Society policy. Despite repeated attempts to get the manager to remove the objectionable material (especially a book by Robert DePugh, leader of the paramilitary Minutemen) he steadfastly refused to adhere to the approved list of books. We had no choice but to revoke permission to use the name American Opinion and to notify the press.

Checking into the situation further, I discovered that our manager had been passing out copies of the viciously anti-Semitic book, *Pawns in the Game*, had loaned racist hate song records produced by the American Nazi Party, had reportedly threatened to send a gang of goons to beat up a reporter unless he wrote a good story about the book store, and had attempted to recruit customers into DePugh's new group, The Patriotic Party. We finally revoked his membership in the Society.

Just weeks before this episode, I was forced to cancel the membership of another person who was in the same chapter. This man was in the KKK and had been identified as such on television. He denied his Klan membership—God love him—but announced on television that he was proud to be a full-fledged member of the John Birch Society. We weren't grateful for the plug.

Another Miami problem was a doctor who organized the nationally known Committee to Warn of the Arrival of Communist Merchandise on the Local Business Scene. The Birch Society supported his ideas for awhile (in fact,

they helped make his committee nationally successful),
but eventually ended the support when other projects
seemed more important. The doctor was one of the early
Birch leaders and tried hard to work himself into a position where he could run most of the Birch activities in
Miami. He resigned from the Society on June 8, 1965
after his power play was squelched.

However, his memory lingers on, and so does his technique for holding "card parties," or economic raids on
local retail stores. Members of his committee search the
shelves for merchandise from Communist countries.
When such merchandise is discovered the raiders infiltrate the store as customers and then fan out to hide little
cards that congratulate whoever buys the material for
supporting "slave labor."

The good doctor is also "noted" for his campaign
against Polish hams, distribution of notices that anybody
who smokes Camel, Tempa, Winston or Salem cigarettes
smokes "Communist tobacco," and for Spanish literature
depicting a can of Budweiser beer decorated with a hammer and sickle (Budweiser once bought a small quantity
of hops from Yugoslavia).

For a time the Society was extremely successful in
attracting Cuban refugees to its anti-Communist program.
On one occasion anti-Castro Cubans joined forces with
some Birch members to picket the Navy recruiting offices
in Miami. They were protesting Navy interference with
exile raids against Cuba, and carried signs proclaiming:
"Enlist in the U.S. Navy, Then Wait for Castro's Orders";
"Et Tu, JFK"; and "After Co-Existence, No Existence."
Few people in the area were aware that the Navy was the
target of the demonstration. A stock broker, while com-

ing out of his office adjacent to the Navy office, asked innocently, "What have you folks got against the Stock Exchange?"

Eventually it became evident that the Cubans were interested in the Society from the standpoint of Cuban liberation. At meetings they would sit patiently through all the talk about educational programs and letter-writing campaigns, and then ask soberly, "When you get us guns so we bomb Havana?" When we made it clear that we were strictly an educational army and had no intention of setting them up for an armed invasion, most of the Cubans lost interest in attending study meetings and reading their Birch *Bulletins*.

Of the various kinds of people that I worked with for the Society, the group which gave me the most difficulty was fundamentalist preachers. I probably just had a string of unusually bad luck, but I ran into preachers who were thieves, perverts, con men and publicity seekers. Once I was about to appoint a man who billed himself as "The Patriotic Pastor" to the chairmanship of a three-county Support Your Local Police Committee. He was anxious for the job and it seemed the perfect way to gain support from community leaders and respectable, church-going citizens. Fortunately, I got a tip from another minister that I ought to check with the police department. I did. At first they were reluctant to part with any confidential information. But when I told them The Patriotic Pastor was about to be the community leader of a committee to support the local police, they had the file sent up quickly and let me in on some shocking information. It seems that "The Patriotic Pastor" had been hauled in for questioning on three separate occasions for molesting little girls. When I had dinner with the pastor that evening, he agreed to resign from the committee.

Another preacher, who was a former classmate of Robert Welch and a Birch chapter leader, attracted a dedicated and affluent following by insisting that according to the Bible God was foursquare in favor of segregation.

Many preachers went to great lengths to win over and cash in on the ready-made Birch congregation. One reverend named his church after John Birch, published a pamphlet about the life of John Birch, held periodic patriotic rallies, sold right-wing literature at the rear of the church and went on a national speaking tour for the Birch Society's anti-civil rights crusade.

Catholic Birchers were overcome with grief when the late Monsignor J. D. Conway, national religious columnist, raked the Society over the coals of hell and said that any Catholic who is a Bircher should examine his conscience. "The stench which emanates from that Society," he said, "can only come from something foul within it." Similar adverse comments from any religious source precipitated a rash of phone calls to my house, as though I had a hot line to the Vatican, the National Council of Churches, or David Ben Gurion.

There was one lady who wore her religion on her sleeve—in fact she boasted about her "fervor" incessantly —who eventually helped cause the complete mental breakdown of a fine woman with an adoring husband and eight children. This zealot had a persecution complex. She was convinced that one of our members was a Communist double agent and was telephoning vile threats to her house. Her paranoia spread like a plague and, in time, the mother of eight children imagined that

78

some other Birchers were trying to ruin her religion and her health. Within two months she feared that her husband was plotting to kill her and that the maid was going to kidnap the children. Finally she was confined to a hospital ward. Her psychiatrist concluded that the breakdown was caused by her Birch activities and a great fear of an imminent Communist takeover.

Liquor has never been much of a problem for the Birch Society in the South since most members tend to frown on drinking. But there are exceptions. I once gave a presentation to a house full of prospects and had to compete with the inebriated hostess who laid on her bed in another room and shouted such remarks as the spirits moved her. As the presentation proceeded she began to mimic everything I said. She laughed hysterically throughout the hour and a half of Robert Welch. Since it was her house there was little I could do except bite my lip, put on as nice a smile as I could under the circumstances, and pray to God that her husband would come home soon and beat the hell out of her.

On another occasion at the same lady's house (I'm a glutton for punishment) we waited in vain for prospects to arrive. When the starting time came and the guests didn't, she blandly informed me, "Oh, by the way, I didn't have time to call and invite anybody." I muttered softly to myself as I disassembled my readied projector, took down my screen, packed up my books and films, and carried them all back to the car for the 25-mile drive home.

Unauthorized literature was the source of a never-ending series of problems. One chapter leader, a doctor of some standing, was infuriated with one of his members who sent out little packets of material to prominent persons and signed his name. The primary piece of literature was a shoddy screed about the famous Selma, Alabama march. It was published by some racist organization and it was entitled "The Urinators."

Perhaps the funniest people of all are the little old ladies—usually long-time members of the Society—who are preoccupied with speculations about the exact date for the Communist takeover they expect any day now. One woman, for example, spent a half-hour giving me instructions on how to flee into the Everglades, what to pack on an air-boat and how to survive in the wilderness. These are the same kindly great-grandmother types who get all excited about mental health programs, firearms control legislation and fluoridation. It was always difficult to convince them that if the Communists decide to attack us, it is very doubtful they'll do it through our water supply. Some of these ladies lose all hope, and even sell their homes and businesses to move abroad.

Surely the world would be a much duller place without the John Birch Society.

6

Saying and Doing
the "Right" Things

Being the man from John Birch wasn't all excitement and publicity. There were myriads of conventional tasks which, although never completely dull when coupled with Birchism, were relatively routine and monotonous. The most wearisome duty of all was the eternal chore of every businessman: correspondence.

Still, exchanging letters with the headquarters of the John Birch Society is far more interesting than reporting on sales meetings or production schedules. Pen pals in Belmont conjure up dilemmas with leftist spies, traitors and what Welch calls "agent provocateurs."

Since I had very little direct supervision (I met only twice in two years with my superior—The Superpatriot) I was duty bound to report regularly and thoroughly to the big Birchers in Belmont. My letters "home" were perpetually optimistic about the inevitable prospects for growth in my territory, and perpetually pessimistic about the conditions under which I had to perform. Most of my dispatches pleaded for patience with our delayed progress as I was hindered by horrendous treatment from the press, sabotage from our enemies and idiocy from our members, the last of which didn't have to be imagined.

But just at the end of the next rainbow I promised a never-ending phantasmagoria of new chapters, new front committees and limitless sales of books, records and bumper strips. A successful day at my typewriter always gave me a peaceful night of happy dreams—visions of the whole staff in Belmont drooling over my latest communiqués from the field.

I especially enjoyed inserting long passages of idle chitchat between the infrequent flashes of hot news. During the winter I delighted in reminding the proud Yankees cooped up in their cubicles in icy Massachusetts how warm and wonderful it was on the sunny Florida Gold Coast. The beaches and warm breezes would be great, I teased, if only I wasn't such a dedicated patriot who sacrificed weekends and evenings to the never-ending struggle for Birch truth, right-wing justice and the American way.

The ballyhoo worked well. When the snow began falling up North, I could count on a steady migration of Birch big-wigs coming south on trumped-up Birch business to take their place in the sun. Northern snow meant that suddenly bookstores needed checking, speakers needed scheduling, committees needed counseling and members needed prodding.

Devising new adverse conditions for letter writing was

something of a game I invented to flaunt my determined devotion to my job. Corresponding at early hours in the morning was kid stuff, I figured, if I could create epistles on motel stationery while eating breakfast on the run at seven in the morning after only four hours of sleep.

I outdid myself once when I was caught at home with hurricane warnings posted. I shuttered and boarded my house. Then, as the winds picked up and the electricity went out, I settled down comfortably with typewriter and candles to give Belmont a gust-by-gust account. Between recapitulations of the victories and defeats of our chapters for that week, I gave a breathless account of coconuts battering the house and the flight of my garbage cans as they were hurled down the street and crash-landed in a ditch. Then, as a broken shutter smashed against the house and broke a window, I signed off with something like this: Better go now; the water is seeping in and our children are frightened. It amused me to hope that the people in Belmont envisioned me cringing miserably in the corner of my leaky house, up to my armpits in water while keeping my children together with one hand and dutifully typing my weekly report with the other.

I feel certain no other Birch coordinator ever topped that one, except perhaps the patriot in Indiana whose home was fire bombed by vandals—although I sincerely doubt that he had the foresightedness to dash off a letter to Belmont while someone else was beating down the flames.

One of my most perplexing problems was soothing distant chapter leaders who feared that other chapter leaders were Communist agents deliberately trying to ruin them. Theoretically, chapter leaders weren't sup-

83

posed to know each other or to communicate with anyone in the Society except their section leader or coordinator. This rule was designed to prevent Communists from infiltrating the Society, getting acquainted with Birchers in as many chapters as possible and then debilitating the entire Birch structure in a wide area by leading the members into meaningless projects. The real effect of the policy, however, was to raise everyone's curiosity to a fever pitch and strengthen their determination to know all the gossip about everybody and everything within a 500-mile radius.

Not infrequently, chapter leaders would become jealous of each other and then escalate the friction until each imagined himself the victim of one of the "agent provocateurs" whom Welch assured the members were constantly creeping up on the Society. These sibling rivalries would then deteriorate into global correspondence conflicts, with letters being fired off to both Belmont and my house from all sides. Defamations would fly in all directions as I diplomatically tried to arrange a cease fire and prove that their worst suspicions were merely imagination running wild. Sometimes I ran amok in these muddy skirmishes and wound up taking cover myself, as one or the other side accused me of being a cleverly planted Communist aiding and abetting Insiders who had penetrated the inner chambers of Birchism.

In these times that tried my soul, our members would clamor, beg and petition for a mass meeting of all Birchers in the area. But Belmont lived in mortal fear of this, knowing full well that any such assembly could easily be provoked into open revolt. Family spats among leaders sometimes decimated entire memberships of the involved chapters and were a chief cause of sizeable Birch defections.

My letters to members were, for the most part, just individual pep talks to spur them on to greater triumphs. My technique was to take the same projects that I glorified in reports to the home office as being the utter salvation of our republic, and belittle them in letters to the members as not being nearly enough to bring lasting progress without much more follow-up activity. At other times members needed to know how valuable they were to the cause of Americanism and how much we appreciated their efforts. Some members wanted the Society to issue certificates and plaques of merit which they could admire in the privacy of their bedrooms.

Sometimes I had to convince leaders that they should split up their growing chapter into two or three separate units. They were usually reluctant to do this, preferring a huge, unmanageable group to sharing their empire with new chapter leaders. One egotist had such a colony of Birchers in his house that it became necessary to rent a restaurant in order to accommodate everyone at the monthly meeting. According to the leader, no one else was competent to run a chapter—which didn't speak too well for the quality of his recruiting efforts.

Communication from Belmont to patriots in the field was very poor—especially when the news was bad. The staff frequently learned of significant Society developments from the news media or telephone calls from members who just heard startling news on TV. When PR men John Rousselot and Tom Davis resigned their positions, the most important Birch defections ever, Belmont didn't even notify the staff so that we could prepare for the resulting morale problems. When I complained about this lack of trust, the answer was that we shouldn't expect to be informed about these matters and, come what may, should simply rely on the people at Belmont. As a coordinator, it was necessary to read the monthly *Bulletin* many times in order to catch any possible clues as to what might be ahead in the way of subtle changes in policy.

Welch also displayed a lack of faith in the membership, for which hardly anyone could blame him under the circumstances. Members frequently felt they weren't getting the real Insider information either from the *Bulletin* or at the monthly meetings. Welch went into the recording business to solve this problem. Beginning in August, 1967 the voice of the master was sent to each chapter on a small 33⅓ record which Welch called a MOM, Monthly Oral Message. But attendance at meetings didn't pick up much and, as a morale booster, MOM soon became a DAD—Dead As Doornail.

Although the Birch Society leaves a lot to be desired from a communications standpoint, it's a whiz at raising money (which isn't easy when you're dealing with conservatives). The Society and its affiliated corporations were taking in $5 million by 1965. Welch thought big and went for $12 million in 1966, but fell so far short that he was begging just to meet his payroll at the end of the year. The Society's Executive Committee put out an urgent appeal which pleaded with all members to "sit right down . . . and send us a check for one thousand dollars." When most members remained standing, Welch admitted to his staff, "The year 1967 has simply been our own 'Valley Forge.'"

86

But as Valley Forge turned into Waterloo, Welch did not sound a retreat with his battered bugle. Instead, with flag held high and drummer boys drumming, Welch marched into another gigantic fund-raising drive. With a crisis slogan of "This Is It!" he sent his 75 professional patriots into the field to extract individual pledges for Continuing Support Clubs. The cost of being a Birch Booster runs anywhere from $10 to $1,000 per month. For $1,000 you can qualify for the Millenium Club (named, no doubt, after the time Welch will reign on earth). A mere $500 per month puts you in the Big D Club. (It has not been revealed what the "Big D" stands for—maybe "Big Dummy.") The Century Club costs $100 per month, and $25 to $50 is enough for the Half and Quarter Century Clubs. Poor Birchers can sneak into the back door of the Sawbuck Club for a measly ten bucks a month.

Welch predicted that without the money the whole operation would soon "fall to pieces." But membership kept declining, big contributors kept disappearing, key personnel continued quitting and internal strife kept increasing. "This Is it!" led to a new slogan: That Was That! And the Society was in the red—a very embarrassing color for Birchers. But being in the red is better than being dead. And like Old Man River, the Birch Society just keeps rolling along. Welch, in fact, says recruiting has taken a decided upswing. He claims the last quarter of 1969 was the most encouraging period in over three years. The Society seems to be growing again.

Raising money was the aspect of being a professional Bircher that I dreaded most. We held periodic fund-raising meetings and attracted an audience by showing a

87

new movie or previewing Birch programs for the year. We also held annual catered fund-raising dinners in the homes of affluent members in each major city. Tom Davis usually flew down to Florida for these, and each dinner brought in from $1,000 to $5,000. Most of the money came from middle class couples making a sacrifice. Birch fat cats seldom coughed up cash or a financial commitment.

Taking Birchers to dinner was also an unpleasant task. It's difficult to enjoy delectable food when your companions are baying about Communist atrocities in the Congo or conjecturing about the numerical strength of alleged homosexuals in the State Department.

Take a Bircher to lunch sometime. While you're looking around for a waiter, Benny Birch is looking around too. "Look at all these people," he'll say. "They're eating and drinking and enjoying themselves as if the country isn't being taken over by the Communists." As you submerge into your soup, he surfaces with a new topic. "About our navy . . . what did you think of the Pueblo case?" When the main course arrives, he'll pontificate on the economy. "I can remember when a meal like this used to cost . . . then along came F.D.R. and inflation and we've been going downhill ever since . . . And what about the gold drain?"

As the meal gets colder, Benny Birch just begins to warm up. Pretty soon you're sputtering along with him, like a couple of dirty spark plugs. And Benny doesn't speak low. Oh, no. As long as he's going into his act, he might as well wake up everyone around him to the worldwide Communist menace. "And while we're at it, why don't we give some literature to the waiter and the cashier. They look like they ought to be Birchers." Undaunted by nasty looks at ringside, Benny continues: "And the colored cook—maybe we could send back *Color, Communism and Common Sense* for him. They don't know it yet, but the Birch Society is the best friend they ever had."

The best friends I ever had in my neighborhood were beside themselves when they discovered "that lovely man with those beautiful children" worked for the John Birch Society. "Can you imagine, a Bircher right here in our neighborhood," they chortled to each other. Nothing that exciting had happened since a minister's son ran away with a divorcee who lived down the street.

There were a number of things which I wasn't obliged to do as a Birch coordinator, but felt I ought to do to bolster morale. For instance, on Sundays I went to a Catholic Church to worship and to a Baptist Church to be seen by all my close Birch friends. The sermons at this particular church were right-wing harangues and it was just like attending a chapter meeting. I didn't participate much, but the members liked to see me there and my attendance bolstered unity. Birchers who prayed together, stayed together. And I needed all the help I could get to keep my chapters happy and humming.

I also felt compelled to stay abreast with the membership in letter writing. The monthly Birch mass production of letters singlehandedly reduces the post office deficit by a sizeable amount. Letters we were directed to write to Congressmen didn't matter much to me personally. Nobody would know whether I wrote them or not—including the Congressmen, to be sure. But letters to editors were a different matter.

Birchers were exceedingly proud of themselves whenever they appeared in print. On the rare occasions when a member hit the jackpot by placing copies of one standard letter in several newspapers at once, there was real cause for celebration. Birchers often carried their letters around with them, whipping them out for a recitation any time they could corner a crowd. One man used to punish me mercilessly whenever I attended a meeting of his chapter. When the business was over and we retired to the parlor to shoot pool, he would doggedly follow me around the table while rendering dramatic readings of his month's production of miscellaneous diatribes.

I managed to match the literary accomplishments of most members with relative ease since I was a fairly good writer. While they were laboriously composing an average of ten letters in order to get one published, I succeeded in placing every letter I ever wrote. This saved me considerable time and embarrassment.

Books have always been an important part of my life. One of the hardships of being a professional right-winger was a self-imposed dictum against buying frivolous reading matter, especially if tainted with liberalism. When prowling through book stalls an inner voice (Welch's, I think) warned me to look with disdain on volumes that weren't on conservative reading lists. I also found myself hiding leftist books in the racks by pushing them behind piles of more acceptable books. Naturally, if I spotted a book by Buckley, Goldwater, Taylor Caldwell, Ayn Rand or any other conservative champion, I would put it in a place of honor where it could be found and fondled by the deprived book-buying public. If the book store had a decent selection of right-wing propaganda (more than two books), I would faithfully troop up to the manager and congratulate him for carrying the "right" things.

Reading is important to every right-wing patriot. It is so important, in fact, that Birchers would walk a mile for an ancient copy of a McGuffey Reader for their children. They do not appreciate the modern educational emphasis on teaching children to get along together. Patriots like sermons and Horatio Alger stories that pound home the marvels of capitalism.

7

My Flag is Redder,
Whiter, and Bluer

One of the prerequisites of being a professional patriot is to remember every conceivable occasion to honor country and flag. Birchers, in particular, are fastidious about a seemingly endless parade of ritualistic patriotism. Since Birchers devote much of their time to outdoing each other in competitive patriotism, a professional must put up a good front in this area in order to earn his pay. This means being in the vanguard of all flag flying, chauvinistic song singing, and historical verse reading.

This presented tremendous problems for me. I'm not particularly strong on stirring renditions of tear-jerking ballads. Right-wingers go into little orgasms of delight over these things.

However, I did try my best to perform all the proper rites and uphold the full liturgy of patriotism. My first problem was a flagpole. I didn't have one. Every self-respecting lover of Robert Welch and the mother country ought to have a flagpole for his very own front lawn. Common citizens can get by with flag brackets or standards, but that simply won't do for the typical public-spirited Bircher. A flagpole it had to be, so a flagpole I got. I bought one from a Bircher friend who went door to door for orders and manufactured custom-made flagpoles in his garage.

Next came the flag. Two kinds of flags are acceptable. You can hold your head up high with either an immense one that is new, bright and clean, or with the sort of flag that would inspire Francis Scott Key by dawn's early light —time-worn, ragged and proud. Anything in between these extremes might necessitate an apology. Birchers are fond of embarrassing you before your friends by announcing that flags are cleaned free by many dry-cleaning establishments as a public service, a fact which wins the unswerving patronage of all local patriots.

My flag, I was proud to say, was redder, whiter and bluer than any flag on my block. But it still took a back seat to other flags in my area. One man had a six-story pole with an immense flag that could be seen waving triumphantly over split-level developments for two miles. Another Birch leader illuminated his flag with spotlights at night and broadcasted the "Star-Spangled Banner" throughout the neighborhood on holidays.

On the Fourth of July, Veterans' Day, Memorial Day, Washington's Birthday and other patriotic commemorations, teams of Birchers would drive up and down streets jotting down the addresses of houses where the colors were being flown. Researching the homeowners' names from a cross-reference directory, Birch chapters would send these people personal letters congratulating them on their patriotism and suggesting that perhaps they ought to channel their feelings into the "constructive" activities of the John Birch Society.

Other patriots worked at encouraging merchants and banks to hold contests, with prizes going to homeowners for such things as most consistent flag flying, most prominent patriotic displays, most authentic representation of an Early American theme.

Right-wingers are fanatically devoted to manufacturers, stores and movie stars who support the American flag. One woman became something of a right-wing celebrity by loyally buying the dog food produced by a right-wing California manufacturer. The fact that she didn't have a dog didn't faze her in the least.

A bank in Tampa sponsored a movie on television that featured Ronald Reagan talking about the American Republic. The Birchers went to work and sent scores of congratulatory letters to the bank, which made them think the program was the all-time champion in audience response. The bank was so pleased that they repeated the entire hour-and-a-half program at tremendous cost.

Senior citizen patriots, who didn't care to endanger life and limb driving around town checking flags on national holidays, often put their creative efforts into composing letters to TV executives in order to try to persuade them to produce patriotic spectaculars. These older people became enraged with their favorite star, Lawrence Welk, when his Independence Day program turned out to be just another summer rerun. The oldsters, of course, wanted Yankee Doodle Dandees, fireworks and battle hymns for the Republic.

Next to having my projector poop out at a presentation meeting, my greatest fear was that some day I would unexpectedly be called upon to fold a flag in public. Never having been a boy scout, a veteran or a post office employee, I just didn't know the proper protocol for folding a flag. What's more, I was too embarrassed to ask someone how to do it. I often imagined how humiliating it would be to be found out. A patriot not knowing how to fold his flag is comparable to Beau Brummel not knowing how to tie his tie.

Birchers didn't stop at flying flags from their homes and yards. They also flew them from the aerials on their cars. Since the little aerial flags flew off easily and were frequently stolen by motorcyclists, Birchers bought miniature flags by the dozens. They also exhibited the flag on heavy-gauge steel reflector license plates and wore flag jewelry and gold-plated Birch leaf pins. (The latter was the closest most Birchers would come to publicly admitting their Society membership.)

Patriotic handkerchiefs were also popular for honoring the colors. One of my best Birch friends was a flag waver to the very end. He went to his grave with a gaudy red, white and blue handkerchief flowing majestically from the breast pocket of his burial suit.

Patriots dearly love to be in parades. They love to dress up in smart-looking Revolutionary War costumes, bandage themselves like war heroes and march to the roll of snare drums and the strains of Dixie. In part, this is just good self defense. I've yet to meet Birchers who were

95

willing to parade sans uniforms or slogans on their own merits as an organization. Instead, they prefer to drape themselves and their floats in flags, impersonate the Founding Fathers, or carry wreaths decorated with the names of American soldiers killed in Vietnam. It is always interesting to watch the reaction of the crowds as Birchers troop by nervously glancing out of the corners of their eyes. The spectators never know whether to boo the Birch Society, or cheer for the George Washington, Patrick Henry and Paul Revere they try to represent.

The need to play the complete role of a patriot extends even to household furnishings. The rise in popularity of Early American furniture was a boon to Birchers; for once it put them smack in the middle of the mainstream of contemporary American taste and fashion. When I took my job with the Birch Society I practically pledged my life, fortune and sacred honor to the patriotic way of life. This included going Early American at my earliest possible convenience. Although Colonial houses are not exactly compatible with Florida architecture, I did manage to buy a ranch house that had white pillars, a fake oil lamp, and some brickwork in front.

Not wishing to spend much money on Early American furnishings (and not having much money to spend), my wife and I improvised a bit and came up with acceptable colonial decor. I painted the largest wall in my living room blood red and hung a huge, angry eagle flanked by the inevitable framed, parchment copies of the Declaration of Independence, the U.S. Constitution, the Articles of Confederation, a Don't-Tread-On-Me flag and a political cartoon with the caption "To hell, Hull, or Halifax," the meaning of which has always escaped me.

96

Robert Welch—He wishes to be remembered as the founder of the John Birch Society. (PHOTO BY FABIAN BACHRACH)

The Birch Society planned to hold civil rights seminars throughout the nation as a way of stopping the civil rights movement. The seminars were to be sponsored by front groups, such as Parents for Racial Harmony. Responsible civic leaders outside the Society were to be enlisted in this cause without their knowledge that the Birch Society was behind it all. The plan was kept very secret and Birch coordinators pushed the campaign quietly without a hint of information published in the *Bulletin* or anywhere that might have tipped off the press. The seminars never amounted to much because few local Birch groups cared to cough up several thousand dollars to put it over. Below is a suggested newspaper advertisement included in the total seminar package deal. Notice that three Negroes are used as the star attraction of this Birch road show.

JULIA BROWN—former F.B.I. undercover agent who spent nine years in the Communist Party and has intimate knowledge of the Civil Rights fraud.

LEONARD PATTERSON — former high-ranking Communist official who was trained in Moscow in the very revolutionary tactics being employed today.

LOLA HOLMES — former F.B.I. informant until 1963 when she testified before the House Committee against Claude Lightfoot, a national leader of the Communist Party.

JULIA BROWN   LEONARD PATTERSON   LOLA HOLMES

Are you confused about all of the recent agitation and violence under the deceptive phrase "Civil Rights"? To learn the truth come to The Conservative Civil Rights Seminar.

A
CONSERVATIVE
CIVIL RIGHTS SEMINAR

SPONSORED BY

Robert Welch, left, talks with the author, Gerald Schomp, in 1966. This was the first opportunity for the author to get to know Robert Welch and marked the beginning of a growing disillusionment with Welch's leadership. (PHOTO COURTESY OF THE SUN-SENTINEL)

Robert Welch strides to the podium to deliver a major address in Ft. Lauderdale, Florida on May 19, 1966. Welch is not a talented public speaker. He frequently reads to his audiences, sometimes for hours, from one of his many pamphlets. Welch is also very nervous. On this occasion when he spotted a photographer positioning himself for a shot from the side, Welch stopped his speech and rebuked the man for interrupting him. (PHOTO COURTESY OF THE SUN-SENTINEL)

The author occasionally spoke to civic clubs about the activities of the John Birch Society. These were usually quite lively affairs and attracted an undue amount of attention from the press. (PHOTO COURTESY OF THE ST. PETERSBURG TIMES AND EVENING INDEPENDENT)

Opposition groups often give the Birch Society credit for more power than they deserve. The AFL-CIO Committee on Political Education, for example, published this booklet on the Society's plan "to take over Congress." Birchers loved it. They reprinted the cover in their *Bulletin* and distributed many thousands of copies of the actual publication as a recruiting tool.

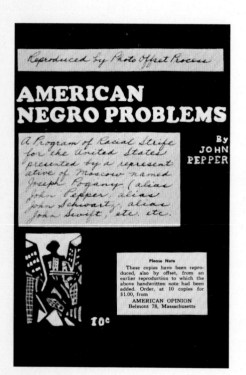

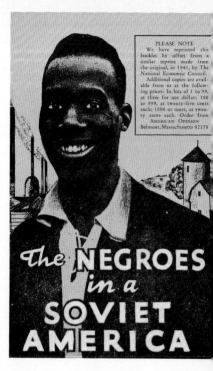

Some of the most widely distributed Birch material is contained in a Civil Rights Packet. These two booklets which the Society relies upon to show that the civil rights movement is a Communist plot were reproduced from original booklets published by Workers Library Publishers in 1928 and 1935. Birchers see a conspiratorial connection between Communist theorizing about revolution by Negroes in the 1920s and '30s and the modern civil rights movement.

On weekends, I painted a gigantic eight-by-six-feet oil painting of a grim George Washington kneeling in the snow at Valley Forge. This pretty much took care of another wall. My wife gathered up all our S & H Green Stamps and claimed a pair of eagle bookends and a Colonial door knocker.

We located a rusty kerosene camper stove at a flea market and converted it into a floor lamp. These few things, along with bright red upholstered dining room chairs, do-it-yourself antiqued furniture and a bookcase full of right-wing books by Robert Welch and other patriots, created an acceptable atmosphere for the numerous meetings, movies and study courses we hosted at our house.

As there are national holidays when Birchers demonstrate extra-extraordinary patriotism (they're never just ordinary in that respect), there are also days when Birchers work hard to "uncelebrate." The most notorious day on the Birch calendar is October 24, United Nations Day. For right-wingers this is a day of national mourning and righteous indignation. There is no symbol more maddening or more provocative to a Bircher than that soft and cuddly UN peace dove. To a Bircher the peace dove is synonymous with the hammer and sickle and the Russian bear.

Right-wing fanatics in every part of the nation watch newspapers closely for advance notices of events commemorating United Nations Day. If a city council or mayor elects to proclaim an official UN Day in their city, right-wing elements deluge newspapers with angry letters to the editor, pressure local politicians to cancel the proclamation and often demand equal time before the

97

city fathers to show their anti-UN filmstrips and argue the case for the Right. If the local UN Association holds public meetings, Birchers sometimes appear there in significant numbers and may even pass out anti-UN literature. Word once came down to me from Belmont that the local post office was likely to allow the sale of UN Christmas cards in their lobbies. Birchers practically frothed at the mouth at this news and immediately went to work demanding equal space in the post office for selling Birch pamphlets.

My second daughter committed the unforgivable sin of being born on UN Day. Birchers were not amused when I told them I planned to christen her Unicef Schomp.

Similarly, members of all right-wing organizations are real kill-joys when the kiddies come around on Halloween to collect contributions for UNICEF. Cartoonists have had a field day poking ridicule at their highly publicized tactic of dropping hate literature that denounces UNICEF as a Communist-front organization into Halloween bags.

I've also noticed that Birchers tend to frown a lot during Brotherhood Week. They don't care for all that talk about universal cooperation and international understanding. One member once challenged the sincerity of the Big Brother movement. To a Bircher "Big Brother" conjures up only one thing: Orwellian impressions of Red comrades in arms plotting against the world.

8

Kooks and Bigots
I Have Known

Since its inception, the John Birch Society, has ceaselessly promoted the idea that it accepts only the finest people into its membership. They have proclaimed time and time again: "We must have associated with us . . . only men and women of good will, good conscience, and religious ideals . . . a body of truly good men and women . . . of all races and colors and creeds . . . The Society believes that improper means are never justified by even the noblest of aims."

Robert Welch and his national conglomeration of men and women of good will are fond of reminding themselves and each other what a great and humane people they are. They feel they are truly God's chosen people and, therefore, crusade relentlessly. They strive to save the inferior Negro from the cruel frustrations of equal rights which are certain to overwhelm the black man in an advanced white society. Birchers are convinced that they have some sort of divine destiny to save America from a United Nations that is just too insidious, secret and clever for us. Birchers are also determined to protect the United States from a top-level conspiracy in our own government which somehow only they have had the foresight to discover. In doing all these things, Birchers seriously consider themselves saintly, sincere, tolerant, dedicated and humane.

My experience as a paid field man for the John Birch Society qualifies me to say that this is totally untrue. I can also say with certainty from experience that the top leadership of the Society deliberately allows bigots, anti-Semites, and ignorant kooks and degenerates to remain in the organization—even when staff members, chapter leaders or good members try to get them out.

U.S. Senator Alan Cranston reported officially when he was California's State Controller in 1966: "The John Birch Society's slip is showing—and showing badly. The slip is soiled and stained with the muck of anti-Semitism and racism, and a smattering of anti-Catholicism." Birchers have been especially enraged by the attacks of the Jewish Anti-Defamation League (ADL) which has been concerned with anti-Semitism in the Society. In order to cope with this touchy problem the Society conceived the brilliant tactical maneuver of rounding up some radical right-wing Jews (who, believe me, are hard to come by) and forming The Jewish Society of Americanists in order to very effectively fight the charge that the Birch Society is anti-Semitic.

Belmont also sent out one of their top public relations

men, personable Tom Davis, to tour the country giving an anti-Anti-Defamation League speech which strongly suggested that the League itself generated a substantial amount of anti-Semitism by harassing the right-wing movement. Mr. Davis was reluctant to make this speaking tour, knowing full well that the Society's allegations were preposterous. I personally showed him a press release that Belmont was sending out to publicize his speeches. It made the silly but serious boast that rather than being anti-Jewish the Birch Society was actually the best friend the Jewish people ever had. This was too much for even battle-scarred Davis to absorb. He hit the ceiling, called Belmont and angrily demanded that they eliminate that "ridiculous statement." It marked the end of his speechmaking on the Anti-Defamation League. When Davis got back to Welch in Belmont he refused to carry out that assignment any longer. Not much later, after nearly seven years as a professional Bircher, he resigned from the Society.

I was happy to see the formation of a Jewish Society of Americanists, even though it was an obvious public relations maneuver to outwit the ADL. I had always felt the conservative movement had many ideas that ought to be attractive to Jewish businessmen. What totally disillusioned me was the reluctance of Society officials to revoke the memberships of Birchers who openly vented their hatred of Jews as a reaction to the formation of a Jewish affiliate. Consider, for example, this note sent to Birch headquarters by a Miami Bircher:

"I would much appreciate answers to the following questions. (1) How can a Talmud believing Jew practice and

teach the principals [sic] and purposes of the JBS when the
Talmud teaches hate and horrible deaths for my Jesus and
lying to, cheating and stealing from, and mistreatment of all
Christians? (Talmud says 'Christians are lower than cattle').
(2) Do your Jews disavow their Talmud, or will they practice
on us the hate and vile teachings they are commanded to by
their 'religion'? (3) Talmudic Jews are already the top boys
of communism, NAACP, ACLU, etc.—may we expect a
speedy takeover of JBS? We are already badly infiltrated! I
shall expect a speedy reply, hopefully from one of your 'Jewish Society of Americanist' boys. Do not ask me if I am anti-
Jewish. Instead tell me if they are anti-Christian?"

The Society answered this letter and went through the
motions of speaking out against anti-Semitism. However,
the key sentence in their reply was, "We cannot retain
anyone if they decide to *spread* such views." (emphasis
mine.) There's the problem. While the Society has denounced anti-Semitism for public consumption, it en-
dures anti-Semitic and racist members as long as they
don't "spread such views," or publicly embarrass the organization. But by tolerating anti-Semitic and racist
views within the membership, Welch practically insures
that such views will ultimately be disseminated to more
members.

Both the coordinator before me and I notified Belmont
leaders about the extent of anti-Semitism in Miami. We
asked that the memberships of such people be cancelled.
But all of this came to no avail. I finally put this issue
firmly on the line in an all-or-nothing letter. Pertinent
parts of the letter went like this:

"Miami is a Jewish city. For every action that Jews take
as a group, there is an opposite and equal reaction from those

in the minority who tend to blame all their own problems on the Jews. As anti-Jewish attitudes of individuals are developed, or irritated to the action stage, there is a seeking out of organizations which are reputed to be anti-Semitic . . . we have thus become the goal of every discontent who's looking for a haven for his couped up hatred. Unfortunately, quite a few of these people were admitted to the Society back in 1964. They, in turn, brought others in. Quite frankly, the Society in Miami *is* now basically anti-Semitic.

"Good prospects and members are quickly disillusioned with the Society. Anti-Semitism isn't something that is inactive, stagnant or secret for long. Anti-Semites, I've found, are quick to tell you that their feelings against Jews are strictly personal and that they wouldn't think of forcing their opinions or prejudices on others. Actually, however, they yearn for the first opening to tell the new member or greenhorn anti-Communist that while we have to fight the Communists, the Jewish Conspiracy is really behind it all. Before long *Pawns in the Game* or some other such garbage is carted out and the matter ends in either of two ways: (1) We soon have another anti-Semite in the ranks, or (2) the member or prospect is disgusted with what he has found in the Society and finds some excuse or pretext to silently fade away from our movement. The end result, then, is that we're getting the kind of people we definitely don't want and invariably losing the kind of people we do want. Consequently, our quality gradually gets lower and, inevitably, our recruiting sinks to a lower and lower level.

"We need to sever relations with *all* the anti-Semites, kooks and defeatists. They're killing us in every way . . . The people we must get rid of aren't helping us much anyway—not to belabor all the harm they're doing. All they *do* is make a bad impression, hate Jews, demoralize good members and completely ruin any chance of recruiting good people. When you really get to know them, most of these people are plainly disgusting—although, of course, most of them pretend to be great Christians."

I asked permission to kick the kooks and bigots out of the Society. Revoking someone's membership is a simple thing to do. The Society's application blank, which each member has signed, reads: "If my application is accepted, I agree that my membership may be revoked at any time, by a duly appointed officer of the Society, without the reason being stated. . . ."

The response was more double-talk and excuses. The answer, buried in verbiage, was that "knowing how bad the problem is there, we still cannot get into the business of 'wholesale expulsion' but simply must try to *save* the good people from falling into this trap of anti-Semitism." The response also said that while the Society would terminate the memberships of "agitators who are hurting the Society," we should take every precaution not to do this "when the individual is a good patriot in every sense of the word." In my estimation, bigots don't make "good patriots" in any sense of the word.

A member who was moving into my area wrote to Belmont headquarters, admitted she was prejudiced against Negroes and took the initiative in resigning for the sake of the Society's image. In her letter she stated: "Under the circumstances, I think the best decision is for me to go on working hard for all the things the John Birch people are striving for, but not to be a formal member . . . if my very strong feelings in the Negro situation might do you harm, and I have been perhaps indiscreet in expressing them to the community at large,

104

it is better to separate myself." This woman advised the home office that she had, in fact, left her home state in New England because of the liberal civil-rights legislation in force there.

I received a letter from headquarters informing me that if after contacting this woman I felt it was best to drop her from our membership (she had already resigned!) I should so advise them. *But,* the letter stated, "if you think it would be worthwhile to attempt to persuade her to continue as a member, by all means do so." Thus the Society not only failed to try to eliminate prejudice among the membership, but actually encouraged people who wanted to resign from the Society because of their bigotry to remain members.

It used to be maddening to have to follow orders from Belmont to bug Birchers who had resigned from the Society in an effort to persuade them to rejoin. My idea was to build a dedicated, elite, national task force made up of only those members who could constantly prove their worth to the Birch cause. But the Birchers in Belmont apparently hated to lose a member and his dues more than they hated the Supreme Court.

They never let a member get away without letters by the score and personal calls from chapter leaders, section leaders and coordinators. Even if this didn't do the trick, Belmont would keep old members on the rolls and send them a monthly *Bulletin.* My wife, for example, has not paid dues or attended a meeting in well over three years; yet, as of this writing, she continues to receive a *Bulletin* every month without fail.

Many times I had to calm angry leaders who had sent in resignations from old members, or dropped inactive members from the rolls, only to discover months or years later that officials in Belmont still carried the names on official rosters and wanted to know why the dues money wasn't being collected. Official membership rolls in the Society are padded with thousands of members who haven't been to a single meeting in years and would be terribly upset to know they are still listed as members of an extreme right-wing organization.

There was one case that serves as an excellent example of how hard it is to quit the John Birch Society. A young family man, who I shall call Don, was fanatically and sincerely devoted to fighting Communism in every conceivable way. As a Birch chapter leader he couldn't do enough to promote new projects and resurrect old ones. In time Don was an important leader in two large counties in southeast Florida, encompassing Miami, Ft. Lauderdale, Pompano Beach and Hollywood. He had been a successful businessman, but his job and his income dwindled to practically nothing as he spent days on recruiting and nights speaking and jousting with liberals in public debates.

With bills piling up as Don went deeper and deeper into debt, it suddenly dawned on him that he really wasn't gaining anything except ugly press notices for himself and hundreds of enemies. At this point he also came to realize what a motley assortment of haters, bigots, racists and kooks he was working with. Don suddenly disbanded his chapter, resigned from the Society and retreated back to normalcy and obscurity. Three years later he was still receiving letters from Belmont asking him to resume paying his dues and attending meetings. The last letter from Belmont said Don was still on the membership rolls because they just knew he didn't want to stop fighting Communism.

During this time I was also receiving letters from Belmont. They were urging me to convince Don to rejoin us in our efforts to save our Republic. Just before I finally resigned from the Society (having discovered the same things that led Don to quit) another chapter leader visited Don to check for the umpteenth time whether he really meant to stay out of the Society once and for all. Not especially amused by the visitation, Don concluded the conversation: "You know, you guys really are a bunch of haters." Later, the chapter leader asked me, "I wonder if he really meant that?"

Communication with the rank and file is as impossible as dialogue with Belmont. Talking to a Bircher about civil or human rights is like throwing silly putty into a fan; it comes back rejected, distorted and unpredictably more active. I once helped entertain a crowded restaurant by arguing loudly with two Birchers, one a state representative and the other a businessman, about individual moral and constitutional rights. The argument whittled down to something like this:

Me: Stop me if I'm wrong. As conservatives we uphold the U.S. Constitution and full protection of the rights of the individual even against society as a whole.

Them: Sure 'nuff. We're libertarians and individualists.

Me: As solid supporters of the free enterprise system, we believe that a man's private property is his own treasure and he is at liberty to use it as he wishes.

Them: True! True! We're capitalists. A man's home is his castle. He can do whatever he wants with it as long as he doesn't violate anybody else's rights.

Me: Righto! That means of course that if a man decides to sell his house to a Negro that's his right.

Them: Whoa there! You mean a white man in our neighborhood is selling to a nigger?

Me: Correct! That's his privilege, huh, fellow conservatives and constitutionalists?

Them: He can't do that in our neighborhood!

Me: Why not, fellow Christians and capitalists?

Them: It would ruin the property values of our homes. It's downright immoral!

Me: Immoral?

Them: Certainly. We all have a moral obligation to keep up the property values—to preserve the integrity of the neighborhood.

Me: What about the integrity of the constitutional principle of the individual right of each man to control his own property? What about the rights of the man who wants to sell his own house—to a Negro?

Them: That's different. In that case it's for the common good of everybody that he can't sell his house to a Negro.

Me: Common good? Isn't that something like Communism?

Them: Communism! Are you suggesting we might be pro-Communist? You know damn well we're two of the best Birchers in Florida.

And so they were. Somehow I much prefer honest bigots who admit their hatred openly without dragging in God, Goldwater and the flag.

Don't bother to try to change a Bircher's mind. It's as closed as a bank vault on Sunday. This sometimes even extends to food preferences. An unusually high percentage of right-wingers are health food nuts and most of these refuse to bend to conformity regardless of social consequences.

One comely Birch lady used to show up for meetings at my house with her own sugar-free, chemical-free, germ-free refreshments which she would take to our kitchen to prepare. While the rest of us scavengers snacked on donuts, cupcakes and coffee, she would munch delicately on natural foods like warm honey cake and fruit juices. Other guests would sense my wife's irritation and go overboard on orchids about the store-bought goodies we provided. The health addict would then respond with pointers on how to combat such maladies as indigestion, cancer, leukemia and arthritis with nutrition and exercise.

I once, and only once, made the mistake of accepting an invitation to lunch from one of these health fadists. Having skipped breakfast in order to be on time for an appointment, I was famished when my benefactor pulled up to his favorite health bar. I let him order for me since I was a beginner at eating for figure rather than fortune. Salivating at the tinkle of spoons and forks on china, my stomach erupted into revolution as my eyes settled on what appeared to be my lunch: some sort of parakeet seed, transparent jelly and a thimble of green tea. Being an average glutton, this didn't begin to fill me up. To alleviate my pangs I gambled on an additional order of avocado sherbet, vanilla wafers and some greens that were beyond my imagination. I lost the gamble. My only consolation was a trip to a cafeteria once I ditched my companion. I celebrated with coconut cream pie, heady solace for my first encounter with starvation.

Some of the kooks in the Society take strange stands for conservatives. One long-time section leader believes that Barry Goldwater is a Communist agent—a Jew set up to discredit and demoralize conservatives. His reasoning on the Vietnam issue is equally fantastic. He believes that if we won the war it would be a victory for the Communists. It would make people believe in our government, which he says is already Communist. Therefore, he reasons, we should pull out of Vietnam now—hardly a conservative position. Quite predictably, this man also refuses to accept Jews or the foreign born as members of his chapters.

A wealthy chapter leader, a lady who considers herself to be very religious, had a shocking answer for me when I proudly announced that my wife was expecting our third baby. "Oh, that's awful!" she moaned. "I'll pray that she'll have a miscarriage."

A little old lady in Clearwater, Florida sold her new car and bought a 1957 Chevrolet. She did this because she had heard that since 1958 there have been four sets of keys made for each new car, and that one goes to the Communists.

Another long-time Society leader believes he is followed and his phone is tapped by Communist agents. If you talk to him on the street and a commercial airliner flies overhead, he may hush the conversation and draw close to a building—in case they are somehow recording his conversation from the sky. This presents real problems for him since he lives very close to an international airport. He also thinks people watch his home. He might have a point there. Over his living room sofa there is a large photo of his nude wife.

A lifetime member of the Society (which means that he contributed $1,000) campaigned for LeRoy Collins for governor of Florida. After Collins was elected and didn't take a strong segregationalist stand, this philanthropist became the laughing stock of the area by piloting his boat up and down the river with a large "Impeach Collins" sign.

The more extreme bigots and crackpots who are allowed to remain in the Society have a demoralizing effect on the rest of the members. That is one reason why so many Birchers are secret about their membership. According to Belmont, about four per cent of the members insist that their mail from the home office be sent in a plain wrapper. One of these super-secret members caused me a lot of grief when I first became a professional patriot. I had a devil of a time contacting one of my chapter leaders. Eventually I discovered that she was using an alias and had her mail sent in a plain envelope to the home of another member.

Clearly, Birchers are not proud of the reputation they have earned. But they would never admit that they deserve such a bad name. Quite the reverse. Most Birchers feel they have earned the right to be secretive about their membership because of persecution and harassment from the nation's press.

9

The Great American Martyrs

Birchers believe that the John Birch Society is the most vilified organization in the United States. And, disregarding the fact that they deserve it, this may be the truth.

The Society has been a major source of news and comment since 1961. Some of this has been inaccurate and slanted. Many times the blame for this distortion lies with the Society and its membership. But, whatever the case, the John Birch Society has encouraged unfavorable publicity and used it to advantage. It has been like water to a dying tree; they needed it to grow.

As the press screamed about the extremism of the Birch Society in the early 1960's, membership ranks swelled and the treasury grew fatter. With each new wave of charges about "fascism," "character assassination," "danger on the right," attendance increased at Birch meetings.

In its early history the Society thrived on controversy and denunciation. The curiosity it aroused built the John Birch Society. A persecution complex and the desire to be a martyr to Communism kept the members from leaving it in droves.

Criticism by opponents of the Society is presented to the members as a sign of the effectiveness of the Birch program. The assumption is that liberal organizations—including even the Democrat and Republican Parties—are controlled by Communists and intrinsically evil. Therefore, whatever they're against must be good. It follows in Welchian logic that the Society is on the right path toward defeating Communism. "Since the Communists are screaming," one member said, "we must be stepping on their toes."

Abuse from even middle-of-the-roaders and non-Birch conservatives is met with new kamikaze loyalty oaths by the faithful Birchers. Robert Welch seldom bothers to answer charges. The PR captains of defense just signal the "smear" play, and the team closes ranks and licks the delicious wounds. I used to reflect this attitude myself. When members would phone me all in a dither about the latest adverse comments about the Society, my standard answer was, "It could have been worse. They might not have mentioned us at all."

When right-wing hero Barry Goldwater said that Welch was "intemperate and unwise" and accused him of making "damaging, ridiculous and very stupid statements," Birchers didn't stop for a minute's reflection.

They assured each other that Barry had "gone over to the other side."

The same thing happened when top Republican leaders launched a cautious attack in 1965. Senator Thurston Morton charged that the Society was trying to infiltrate the GOP and insisted that the Party had no room "for a clandestine organization engaged in character assassination." Senator Everett Dirksen said about the same thing, and so did Representative Gerald Ford of Michigan. Robert Welch had a clever answer which tickled the nervous Birchers no end. He said the charge the Society was trying to steal the Republican Party was ridiculous. "We don't indulge in petty larceny," he retorted.

The only criticism that really bothers the Birch hierarchy and causes the members to pause momentarily and reflect on their activities is that which comes from Birch staff or Council members who publicly resign from the organization. Although almost all former Birch officials prefer to keep their real reasons for resignation quiet—either because they wish to remain in some aspect of right-wing activity (sometimes for very lucrative returns) or because they are ashamed to publicly admit a foolish mistake and thereby jeopardize their future—occasional derogatory public comment by a former Birch leader sends shudders throughout the entire Birch leadership.

Obviously, a former official member of the Birch organization knows what he's talking about when he criticizes Robert Welch or the Society. He's not just another "prejudiced" liberal taking potshots from the outside for the benefit of what Birchers call the "anti-anti-Communist" movement. In this situation, the Belmont head-

114

quarters can not rely on its usual blanket boast that the criticism demonstrates how effective the Society is. There are only two weak choices open for explanation to the curious membership: either the man was a planted Communist or Insider infiltrator (which raises questions about the security of Birch personnel policies and makes members even more nervous and suspicious than they normally are), or the staff member was disgruntled about his own personal or financial situation within the Society (which causes speculation that someone who was held in high esteem by the normally super-cautious Birch authorities and trusted with knowledge of the Society's inner workings might indeed have reason to find serious fault with the organization).

When a few men have left the Birch staff or Council and have been candid enough to publicly admit disagreement with Birch procedures or policies, the Society has tried to imply either or both of these sinister motivations. This effort to discredit criticism for the sake of reassuring the membership usually is not completely successful.

This book represents the first attempt by any former employee of the John Birch Society to both publicly admit his foolish mistake in sincerely embracing the Birch line, and to publicly set the record straight after a long period of reflection without malice, bitterness, or concern with the many possible consequences (either good or bad). It will be interesting to me, and to many Birchers, to see how the Society handles this unprecedented publicity.

Liberals often lose their heads when Birchers go into operation. They sometimes forget that "academic freedom" and "free speech" work both ways in America.

When local Society members attempt to enter a float into a patriotic parade, the town fathers will usually scream bloody murder and give the Birchers more publicity than all the marching bands put together. When Birchers in Virginia put up an "Impeach Earl Warren" billboard, a local dentist got so angry that he trespassed on the property and sprayed "Join the Nuts" over the sign in large letters with red paint. This sort of ill-advised activity gains the Society more national coverage than they could possibly buy on billboards.

Even the Federal Communications Commission handed down a ruling that the Birch Society couldn't qualify as an educational organization for an educational TV license. This was rather ridiculous as the Birch Society wasn't even considering applying for one.

Several national organizations of liberals have been set up solely for the purpose of discrediting the John Birch Society. These groups have unwittingly helped the Society. Society members, in fact, often help distribute the publications of these organizations as a way of demonstrating how effective the Birch Society really is. Birchers got a lot of humorous mileage out of the formation of a local group in Massachusetts known as the Birch Watchers. The Birchers say, "If all these liberals are against us, we must be getting somewhere." As one member wrote in a letter concerning publicity about the Society: "Most are adverse comments. As you may well know this works mostly in our favor." And so it did in the early years of the Society.

The Birch Society is also attacked consistently in the Communist press. Welch points this out to all right-wingers. He said in the March, 1966 *Bulletin,* "We now have the whole Communist apparatus treating us as their chief enemy." The members love to hear this. Everybody on the right wants to be the Communists' worst enemy. But the real reason the Communists attack the Society is because Welch's ludicrous positions consistently leave it wide open for easy slaughter. The Communists, like all good strategists, assault the most vulnerable enemy flank. Of all American institutions, the Society always seems to be spreadeagled and ready for instant martyrdom by the Communists. The Reds are quite content to have the Birchers play the role as the hub of anti-Communist activity. Through them, they have been partially successful in smearing their entire opposition.

Liberal attacks on the Society solidify the bull-headed determination of the most active members to stick with Welch until the bitter end, no matter what fantasy he perpetuates or what new absurdity he proclaims. It has been my experience that an unbelievable number of even long-time members have read few of the Society's basic publications. This lack of knowledge about their own organization and the childlike faith they have in all right-wing propaganda make Birchers susceptible to wild rumors. Many are gullible and fall for the wildest stories that come along—like, for example, Operation Water Moccasin which was reputed to be a UN plot to train African savages in Georgia for a takeover of the United States.

Many chapter leaders believe their phones are tapped. I spent considerable time driving long distances for personal meetings with chapter leaders who refused to talk about details over the telephone. Some members believe they are constantly followed. I must admit that all their suspicions eventually got to me. I began to hear imaginary clicks on my phone. Once when a repairman came to fix my telephone, I stayed with him the entire time to make sure he didn't insert a monitoring device into the mouthpiece. I paid close attention on the road to who and what was behind my car. While conducting presentation meetings out of town, I would take irregular routes back to my motel and linger on stairways and balconies to make sure no one was tailing me.

Some Birchers have developed such intense persecution complexes that they will never be satisfied until they're assassinated by a Communist. It's true, in fact, that some will never accept a victory. They deliberately twist conservative victories into psychological defeats. These unfortunate ones will never rest in peace until they're lined up against a Communist wall and sent at last into a state of permanent bliss with a bullet in the head.

10

Robert Welch
and the Neutralizers

Ever since the Birch Society was founded Robert Welch
has warned the members about various plots to wreck the
conservative cause. He calls the people who set such
nefarious Birch traps "the neutralizers."

Neutralizers come in all forms and sizes. They use a
variety of means and devices to accomplish their ends.
The chief culprits are: anti-Semitism; too much faith in
the power of prayer; Biblical prophecies that Communism is inevitable; democratization; total preoccupation
with political action; the tendency to go off on tangents;
paramilitary activity, and the self-defeatism of thinking
it is too late to do anything to save our country from
Communism.

An examination of Welch and the Society in regard to
these neutralizing agents is in order. Let us, then, exam-

ine the conscience of the "conservative" John Birch Society.

Anti-Semitism—As we have already seen, the Society permits anti-Semites to remain members as long as they don't publicly embarrass the organization.

Over-emphasis on prayer—Welch has never been accused of this. Better Birch than church.

False interpretations of Biblical prophecies—Welch hires his own prophets. He calls them "coordinators" and from time to time gives them his divine revelations.

Democratization—No fault here. Welch does not encourage dialogue or majority rule. The Society is monolithic and Robert Welch is king. He renders all opinions and makes all decisions.

Preoccupation with political action—Hell hath no fury like Robert Welch on politics. Welch scorns politicians, although he once tried to be one.

"Tangentitis"—This is Welch's term for the disease of going off on tangents. He personally refuses to get sidetracked, but Birchers are notorious for tilting at such windmills as mental health, new math and metro or consolidated local governments. Little old Birch ladies are fond of sneaking extraneous literature into American Opinion Book Stores (especially manuals with vivid atrocity pictures showing all the pockmarks you'll get if someone fluoridates the water supply).

Paramilitary activity—Welch has roundly condemned the Minutemen and the Ku Klux Klan. Members of these groups are not allowed in the Birch Society. The rule is strictly enforced by chapter leaders—with paramilitary threats if necessary.

120

Self-Defeatism—Welch says America is already 60 to 80 per cent Communist controlled. But he holds out hope for us. If everybody unites behind him we will still have a one-in-three chance to save our skins.

In the conservative game Welch is way out in right field when it comes to delineating the important issues and planning a strategy for victory. Perhaps the *Dr. Zhivago* fiasco was the first real issue which separated Welch from other right-wing compatriots. Early in 1959 Welch used the pages of *American Opinion* (earlier, he had used the *Blue Book*) to reveal that the famous Nobel Prize novel by Boris Pasternak was an intricate Soviet conspiracy to propagandize Communism. He said that rather than try to suppress *Dr. Zhivago,* as Russia's banishment of Pasternak from Soviet literary circles would indicate, the Communists were merely playing charades for the purpose of tempting the Free World to read it. Welch warned that the book promotes the theme that Communism itself is all right—its only drawback is the character of the current leaders. Other conservatives heralded *Dr. Zhivago* as an anti-Communist novel.

Since then Welch and other right-wing leaders have differed on many issues, primarily in degree rather than substance. Welch wants to abolish foreign aid completely. He says it is used by our Communist government to spread Communism all over the world. Most other conservatives view foreign aid as a massive, mismanaged washout, but still a necessary evil to keep needy countries from turning to Russia for financial assistance. They would become stingy Santas, doling out gifts to only those countries which become our faithful helpers.

Welch would not concede that Communism suffered a serious setback in Indonesia. As he put it, the Indonesian bloodbath was instigated by the Communists themselves in order to get rid of one bungling Communist dictator and substitute another before the people staged a genuine rebellion. The fact that practically every Communist in the country was butchered did not make him modify his bizarre theory at all.

He also sized up the 1956 Hungarian revolution as a Communist trick to lure out and smash rising underground resistance before it became too well organized. Other right-wingers hailed these events as momentous anti-Communist upheavals. They were saddened that the U.S. did not heed the pitiful Hungarian plea for help.

The Birch Society saw President Johnson's intervention in the Dominican Republic crisis of May, 1965 as an attempt by our government to prevent an anti-Communist military victory. Birchers said that President Johnson wanted to pave the way for a Communist takeover via the election of Juan Bosch to the Dominican presidency. When Bosch lost the election, the Society was at a loss to explain how our State Department failed to set up a Communist coup. Other conservatives applauded President Johnson's firm stand.

Clever conservatives play it cool over the Russia-China rift; they're happy about the separation, but are still waiting for the final divorce before they step in to court the Russians. Most conservatives want to drive a permanent wedge between the two former Communist partners.

Some conservatives say that now is the time to liberate China. They want to strike while she is divided and

Russia's friendship for the Chinese is at its lowest point.

As usual Welch disagrees. He insists there is absolutely no split between the two Communist blocs. He calls it "the most deceptive and dangerous fraud of our time"—a ploy to lull us to sleep. (Welch is not completely sure of himself on this one, however. When TV personality Joe Pyne asked Welch if he would resign as head of the Birch Society if he was proved wrong, Welch retorted quickly, "Not necessarily so.")

American Opinion magazine ran a series of articles about the case of Julius and Ethel Rosenberg who were convicted and executed for delivering vital atomic secrets to Russia. The series was climaxed with the conclusion that the Rosenbergs were not guilty, as the Communists had claimed. Welch highly recommended these articles and called them "solid dynamite." They must have been —other conservatives blew up in indignation when they heard about them.

The articles coincide neatly with another Welch premise, which is that the Soviet Union is bluffing us into believing a gigantic myth that they are a major nuclear threat and are ahead of us in outer-space exploration.

This idea, Welch believes, is simply another neutralizer, another means to take American minds away from the internal subversion which will lead to a domestic Communist takeover. There is no need for the Russians to attack us militarily from without, he says. He gives the usual reason: Moscow and Washington are but "two hands of one body controlled by one brain." What else?

Aside from his own intuition (which he often seems to rely on exclusively), Welch's primary source of military information is Dr. Medford Evans, a former administrative officer on the U.S. atomic energy project (1944–1952) and popularly known as a leader of the racist Citizens' Councils of America.

Dr. Evans relied heavily on science writer Lloyd Mallan for material for his most recent expose articles on what he calls the Russian space "hoax." Mallan wrote a book entitled *Russia and the Big Red Lie*, published by Fawcett in 1959, in which he concluded, "The much heralded scientific successes of the Soviet Union in recent years are, for the most part, little more than pipe dreams—the creations of an active, blatant, shameless propaganda machine."

In 1966 Mallan wrote a complete series of articles for *Science and Mechanics* Magazine (later published in book form) in which he presented the following conclusions:

(1) The famous Russian walk in space by Cosmonaut Leonov on March 18, 1965 was a phony—never happened.

(2) The Russians, as of June, 1966, never launched any man or woman into space.

(3) The Russians did not land Luna 9 on the moon or take any pictures of the other side of the moon's surface.

Welch's assumptions on Russian military might are at odds with other right-wingers who preach that our government is playing into Russian hands by disarming our missile and bomber defenses while the enemy is preparing a surprise, annihilating nuclear attack from orbital rockets in outer space. The theory gained credence from the nationally syndicated Allen-Scott Report of June,

1967, which told of orbiting Soviet satellites capable of reaching the United States and launching nuclear bombs at targets across the nation from California to New York. Allen and Scott claimed that prototype satellites of these multi-warhead, independent, re-entry vehicles were sent over the U.S. in 1966 and exploded into a number of pieces on signal. Subsequently, Russian Communist Party Chief Leonid Brezhnev announced that the Soviet Union did indeed possess orbital bombs. Former Secretary of Defense Robert McNamara then admitted that Russia would be capable of raining nuclear warheads on the U.S. from outer space by 1968. Birchers promptly called the whole thing a hoax. Other conservatives shuddered; they believe the doom and gloom boys.

These are fun things compared to the conservative wars fought over Welch's utterances about President Eisenhower and his hawkish Secretary of State, John Foster Dulles. I've already dwelled on the Eisenhower slander. The latest bash concerns the Society's new anti-Dulles book, *The Actor*, by Alan Stang.

The author's fame has come from his only other book, *It's Very Simple*, which is a mish-mash of disjointed quotations and speculations that spell out the Birch line that the civil rights movement is a Communist plot. Stang had a real challenge to top that one. But, unfortunately, he did it. Stang promotes the same sarcastic line that he has used in public speeches: "Conservative, Republican, anti-Communist John Foster Dulles not only was not a conservative, or Republican or anti-Communist . . . but a member and leader of the International Marxist Conspiracy."

There are many other serious, and hopefully fatal,

disparities between Welch and other right-wing leaders. The John Birch Society even neutralizes itself on occasions. Stubborn recruits sometimes ask why the Society uses so many reprints issued by Congressional investigating committees when it is elementary to Birch philosophy that our American government is already controlled by the international Communist conspiracy.

Neutralizers who infuriate Welch the most are other right-wingers who don't agree with him. William Buckley, Jr., in particular, is anathema to the Birch Society. Buckley feels the Society is a menace not only to the conservative movement but to the country itself. His denunciations of Welch send up howls of pain from Birchers all over the country. Many Birchers openly refer to Buckley as a Communist and, worse yet (horrors!) an Insider.

Buckley has been fully acquainted with the Society almost from the time Welch breathed life into it. He attended one of the early Birch presentations in 1959 and, according to someone who was also there, was the only person in a group of about a dozen at the meeting who did not join the Society.

At first Buckley had a few choice, but cautious, words of praise for Welch. Then in 1962 he wrote an editorial which was highly critical of Welch, but not the members of the Society. In 1965 Buckley really lowered the boom in a six-part special section in his magazine, *National Review*. In one of the articles, James Burnham, the author of a number of books (one of which was widely distributed by the Birch Society) made this conclusion: "Responsible conservatives have long tried to believe that the JBS, though 'misguided,' was 'going in the same direction' and therefore an 'ally'. . . . But unfortunately, under the years of brainwashing and organizational control by Robert Welch, the Society as a collective body has taken off in directions where no conservative can prudently venture, and has become a suitable ally only for confusion and sterility. . . . Any American who seriously wants to contribute to his country's security and well-being and to oppose Communism will have to stay clear of the JBS."

Swift reaction from Birchers was painful for Buckley. Welch has boasted that the Society comprised one-third to one-half of *National Review*'s total subscriptions. When the issue hit the mail, Birchers cancelled their subscriptions by the thousands. But Buckley continues to snipe at the Birch Society's program every chance he gets. As he puts it, "One continues to wonder how it is that the membership of The John Birch Society tolerates such drivel." I often wonder how I did it myself.

11

The Birchers Are Coming!
The Birchers Are Coming!

My transition from the world of public relations and advertising to that of a professional patriot was a rude awakening. Never in the history of public relations has there been such an example of outrageous press relations as the John Birch Society.

In the normal course of human events, PR-conscious corporations pander to the press in every conceivable way in order to impress the fickle buying public with their innate goodness. It has been hard, to be sure, but the members of the Birch Society have successfully reversed this time-honored American business tradition. Any press agent worth his credit cards would love to be pursued by reporters and cameramen the way Birchers are. Yet, when the press approaches a Bircher (if one is miraculously identified) he will clam up and refuse to reveal anything about anything—usually not even his own rank and chapter number.

Press representatives are only human. When their legitimate questions about the Society are unanswered or dodged, they rely on the best sources available, even if they are unreliable. When Welch suggests the American press is under Communist control, it is too much to expect that reporters will respond with friendly plugs to aid Welch's recruiting program. When local Birchers inaugurate campaigns of boycott, villification or intimidation against reporters, TV personnel or radio personalities, it is understandable that these people lash back at the Society with vituperation, misquotation and exaggeration.

For example, one Birch section leader crowed about his "victory" over a local radio personality in a letter to the home office. He said that after an extremely effective letter-writing campaign a "left-wing commentator" had lost about 15 of his sponsors and was reduced to raving like a mad man about the Society.

Until I actually met this radio announcer, I also thought he was an escapee from a straight jacket. While discussing the Birch Society on his program, he at times appeared beside himself with rage. He frequently called Birchers "subversive," "mental cripples," "liars," "Fascists," and "intellectual cancers." The announcer also said the *Blue Book* is Welch's *Mein Kampf*, and that thousands of Birch members would like to see the Jews gassed. This Hitlerian connotation is not exactly good PR.

I doubted that I would have much in common with the broadcaster. Yet, when I collected myself, went to see him and listened to his story of intimidation from local Birchers, I was amazed that he treated me as cordially and objectively as he did. I was also flabbergasted to discover that he had once been a conservative and had letters from such right-wingers as Dr. Fred Schwarz, Billy James Hargis, Carl McIntire and Kent Courtney to prove it. Robert DePugh, head of the militant Minutemen organization, admits that it was this same individual who, while serving as an announcer in the Mid-West, had played a great part in inspiring him to be an anti-Communist.

Yet the record of vile and threatening letters sent by Birchers to this man, the incredible letter-writing campaign aimed at his sponsors, the phone calls made to his advertisers and the abuse heaped upon him by phone calls to his station, were absolutely shameful in every respect. One Birch chapter leader found an especially effective way to win his good will. This Birch ambassador would telephone the broadcaster's call-in program and set off a firecracker when he picked up the receiver. All you could hear on the air was the announcer's usual salutation, and then, a gigantic "BLAM!"

Another Bircher, a section leader, sued the same announcer for libel for allegedly calling him a "right-wing Communist." When I threw caution to the wind and arranged to have a Birch national public relations man appear on the radio program, this section leader called me in the middle of the night to warn me that he would resign from the Society unless I cancelled the program. I was overjoyed at this news, as I had been wondering how to get rid of him for months. Unfortunately, after I gave my blessing and hung up, he backed down. He declined to leave our membership, as he was afraid it might interfere with his law suit.

The announcer once invited me out for drinks and a father-to-son sermonette about our public relations program. He said good naturedly that he didn't want to jump to any rash conclusions, but our members just possibly might be going about things the wrong way. When we entered the lounge, obviously a favorite haunt of his, he politely excused himself and made the rounds of all the tables, cattily tipping off his friends that he had dragged in a genuine souvenir of Birch extremism. I was quite a sensation. The best I could manage was a weak smile and a silly half wave as each table full of spectators turned discreetly to get a good gander at a right-wing goof.

As a Birch coordinator I used to work hard to promote a better deal from the press. I often visited newspaper offices to discuss Birch articles with editors and drop off reading matter so reporters would have official Birch philosophy available in their files. Whenever possible, I appeared on interview radio programs so that I could answer questions from listeners. I always earned respect from announcers by simply being candid. But almost invariably all my work would be undone before I had time to leave the station. I got used to the post-program ritual of being politely walked to the reception area by a now more understanding announcer, only to hear an upset switchboard operator's interruption: "Mr. ————, we're getting calls from people who identify themselves as Birchers. They say we're a bunch of Communists!"

The Miami members screamed foul whenever I or any other Birch Representative dared to go on any of the stations they were boycotting. Yet, these same people helped build the audiences of the very shows they hated by staying up all hours of the night to listen in. To top it off, when they got together at meetings, they would compare notes and wallow in self-pity while discussing how terrible it was that they were being persecuted.

The Birchers in Miami boycotted a major television station which is managed by liberal businessmen. The station produced an anti-right-wing program entitled, "The Patriots," which triggered the boycott.

A month later an irate Birch section leader caused an uproar at a Jaycee meeting where he was supposed to speak on the topic, "Why The John Birch Society?" He had agreed to make the talk on the condition that the boycotted television station would not be permitted to film it. When a TV photographer appeared and began taking pictures, the Bircher gathered up his copies of *None Dare Call It Treason* and stormed out of the meeting. On his way to the exit he took a futile swing at the TV newsman who was getting some of the best film footage of his career.

Later, another Bircher printed thousands of flyers which asked why the station was soft on Communism. The station loved all this controversy, of course. It was an unexpected bonanza for their news program ratings. I had to work fast to convince the Birch hotheads that launching a letter-writing campaign against the station's advertisers would only backfire.

A year and a half later, when I accepted an invitation from this station to speak about American freedom for an Independence Day program, Birchers in Miami circulated the rumor that I (their official representative) was a Communist and a traitor.

If any organization has ever needed a public relations genius to polish its public image, that organization is the John Birch Society. To accept this challenge, up stepped John Rousselot, a talented and aggressive former U.S. Congressman from the bedrock of Western conservatism, Orange County, California.

In 1964 Rousselot launched a highly creative campaign to break down some of the antagonism between the Birch Society and the press. Within a year he opened and staffed public relations offices in San Marino, California; White Plains, New York; Dallas, Texas; Chicago, Illinois and Washington, D.C.

The official word went out to the membership and the staff—say absolutely nothing to the press, just refer them to Rousselot in California. Although it made the Society seem to be even more secretive on the local level, at least there weren't as many Birchers insulting reporters. The Society at last had a capable representative who appeared somewhat reasonable to newsmen. It also had men who could immediately correct the most blatant misrepresentations, such as Drew Pearson preposterously reporting that the Birch Society was distributing a bumper sticker which read, "Kill a commie for Christ!"

Rousselot was at his best during the 1965 GOP tirade against the growing power of Society members within Republican ranks. When top Republican leaders took swipes at the Society, Rousselot flashed his masterfully sweet smile and displayed his sarcastic disdain at a nationally reported press conference. "We are delighted that more and more political activists are joining the long, long line of 'Birch watchers.' The pastime of 'Birch watching' is becoming a very popular one. Each time another individual speaks out on this subject, more people come to our meetings, read our material, and join the John Birch Society. It helps our growth tremendously, and for this we are indeed grateful."

When the Republican Coordinating Committee released their statement on the Birch situation, it was a sickly denunciation of extremism in general which did not even mention the Birch Society by name. There were too many big GOP financial contributors who would have been highly offended by anything more specific against the Society.

Rousselot had a field day at the Committee's expense. He said:

The John Birch Society is in agreement with the Republican Coordinating Committee that not only should Republicans, but also all Americans, refuse membership in any radical or extremist organizations which attempt to misuse any other organizations in the country for evil purposes, or which seek to undermine the basic principles of American freedom and constitutional government. It is obvious that the Republican Party did not find the John Birch Society to be in any such category, and therefore refused the hysterical pressures of the radical, left wing elements of its own party to designate The John Birch Society improperly."

Rousselot's main publicity thrust was to attempt to shatter the widely accepted generalizations that had labelled the Society as anti-Negro, anti-Semetic and anti-progress. The widespread impression that the Birch Society is anti-Negro by policy was changed somewhat by the rather obvious PR maneuver of establishing a Negro college scholarship fund named in honor of Manning Johnson, a Negro ex-Communist who spent his later years telling blacks about the Reds. The Society also put a few Negroes on its speakers' bureau and sent them around the country to speak against the civil rights movement.

Rousselot made some progress in convincing the nation's press that the Society's popularity in the South was not caused primarily by white backlash. He made progress for awhile, that is, until the end of 1965 when the speakers' bureau introduced a new lecturer—segregationalist Sheriff Jim Clark of Selma, Alabama. That burst the soft-soap bubbles once and for all.

The idea that the Society is anti-Semitic by intention was countered by the formation of the Jewish Society of Americanists. The group was organized by the few Jews who found a home in the Society. It didn't really accomplish much, except to throw the Jewish Anti-Defamation League into fits of temper which brought a lot of sadistic joy to Birchville in Belmont.

While the PR program wasn't making the Birch Society America's favorite charity, it was at least dispelling the idea that perhaps membership should be a crime punishable by death. Newsmen began to tolerate the Society as an appropriate but harmless place for misfit, right-wing extremists. Some even swallowed it completely. Rex Westerfield, now Birch national director of public relations, reported that in the Southeast alone eleven newsmen joined the Birch Society in the peak PR year of 1966.

The latest important newsman to give aid and comfort to the Birch Society is Herman Dinsmore, former editor of the international edition of *The New York Times*. Mr. Dinsmore has written a public endorsement of Robert

135

Welch's book, *The Politician*, and says it is "the product of historical research of the first order." He has also toured for the Society as an American Opinion speaker. On March 6, 1970, Dinsmore elected to formally become a member of the Birch Society before 2,000 people at the Society's Annual Council Dinner in Los Angeles. Dinsmore remarked to the crowd that he had come "full circle" from what he used to think about the Birch Society. Indeed, he has.

However, there were still gigantic barriers that could not be overcome to make the Birch Society acceptable to the majority of the American people. For instance, the Society never undid the traumatic fear suffered by moderate liberals who thought Birchers were infiltrating practically every American institution. Educational organizations, in particular, would become quite hysterical at rumors of a secret Birch cell in their locale. Welch made a catastrophic blunder in 1961 when he advised Birchers to, ". . . join your local PTA at the beginning of the school year, get your conservative friends to do likewise, and go to work to take it over." Years later, whenever more than the usual handful of faithful sufferers showed up for their monthly meeting, nervous PTA ladies were still shrieking, "The Birchers are coming! The Birchers are coming!"

And Welch's own irresponsible statements could not be wished away and forgotten—especially since he refused to retract any of them. Rather than play down *The Politician*, Welch urged members to distribute it for recruiting purposes. The book was sold in every American Opinion Library and advertised in Birch publications.

Other Welchisms were equally bothersome. Welch's

136

statement that "democracy is a weapon of demagoguery and a perennial fraud" was part of a very unfortunate argument that the United States is a republic, not a democracy. Technically he is correct; but from a practical standpoint, the terms "republic" and "democracy" are now interchangeable in use and meaning. Welch has been debating these semantics for years.

The Scoreboard Issue of *American Opinion* has been another sore point for the public relations department. You can't tell the Communists without a score card, Welch decided. Therefore, in the early days of *American Opinion*, Welch promised that he would publish an annual rundown of the Communist advance around the world. To fulfill this promise, each year a combination July–August issue is dedicated to a capsule summary of the situation in each nation of the world. This is capped off with a special scoreboard which lists an estimated percentage of Communist control for each country. The United States is estimated to be 60 to 80 per cent under Communist control. When Rousselot was at the helm, the Birch public relations department would have liked to close down for a vacation whenever the Scoreboard Issue was published. Tom Davis, who was Eastern public relations manager at that time, usually just admitted that he didn't agree with it and said the whole thing was useless and confusing.

Another bitter pill for the Birchers to swallow was the resignation of Dr. S. M. Draskovich from the Council in 1966. Draskovich is a dynamic Yugoslav publisher who lives in Chicago. Welch called him "one of the five best-informed anti-Communists in the world," until the good doctor quit on him. Draskovich resigned from the Council because of Welch's lack of leadership. He said Welch had "become a dictator, going off on tangents, making irresponsible statements." Now Birchers consider him a pretender to Welch's throne and a suspicious character.

About the same time another Council member, Dr. Revilo P. Oliver, controversial classics professor at the University of Illinois, also resigned. Welch had referred to him as "an authenic genius of the first water, and quite possibly the world's greatest living scholar." Welch's face was quite red when the world's greatest scholar stood up in Boston before the 1966 annual New England Rally for God, Family and Country and announced that the ancient "Jewish conspiracy" was a nucleus of other conspiracies which indirectly led to the "evils of today." Worse yet, when Oliver sat down the applause was thundering. So was the angry reaction from the Jewish community and the press. Dr. Oliver didn't need any new enemies. He had plenty left over from his infamous "Marxmanship in Dallas" article for *American Opinion,* in which he said President Kennedy had been killed by the Communists because he was about to "turn American" and was no longer useful to the planned Communist overthrow of our government.

Welch has a way of going into disputes roaring like a lion and coming out bleating like a lamb. The thorn that caused him the most intense internal pain was a cleaning product known as Swipe. Birchers across the nation were selling Swipe as a sideline. The Society was side-Swiped so quickly, in fact, that many Birch staff men were busily setting up elaborate organizations and using local Birchers as salesmen. When Welch belatedly discovered this

138

competition, he took some verbal swipes at Swipe in the *Bulletin* and in personal letters. By then Birchers had a lot of money invested in Swipe and they didn't care to be cleaned out by Welch. Many chose to stick with Swipe and quit the Society in order to protect their investment.

Welch once got himself into a jam by commenting in the *Bulletin* that he was travelling from city to city in an attempt to straighten out "acrimonious disputes" raging among the members. All he accomplished, Welch said, was to get himself splattered with the oil he was trying to pour on troubled waters. The national press picked this story up with glee and reported that the Society was torn with bitter dissension. Welch immediately denied this; he explained that he was merely trying to be funny. The members weren't laughing.

In 1964 Welch wrote a pamphlet entitled *The Time Has Come*. A headline on the front page of this booklet proclaims, "Washington has been taken over!" The next sentence explains, "By which we mean that Communist influences are now in full working control of our Federal Government." Compound these statements with many similar ones, plus Welch's assertion that the press is almost completely Commie-controlled, and you hardly have a prescription for healthier public relations.

But the members themselves are the biggest liability to the image of the John Birch Society. Nobody will ever persuade them that reporters are not a bunch of ogres who are out to see what color a Bircher bleeds when wounded by a poison pen.

Rousselot and Davis eventually realized they were working against impossible odds. Welch's suspicion of

139

the communications media, his many indiscretions, and the irresponsible antics of kooky members were just too much to overcome.

Robert Welch never could have survived a transition from persecution to relative popularity anyway. His whole thesis that the Society must be good because it is heavily attacked by liberals would have been destroyed if Rousselot had accomplished his goals. Furthermore, if Welch ceased to be a martyr of the press, the membership itself would accuse him of selling out to the "enemy."

John Rousselot parted company with Robert Welch on June 1, 1967. Tom Davis had resigned before him. Three of the Society's five PR offices have been closed. All the PR men were valiant; but nobody could remove the stigma from Welch. He is undoubtedly the worst PR man in American history.

12

A Hell of a Way
to Fight a War

William Tecumseh Sherman said "war is hell." That's doubly true when the war is fought Birch style. Welch has decreed that all good Birchers should come to the aid of the troops in Vietnam. But his manner of backing the boys up front is in such a devilishly conceived, roundabout way that getting to the core of the matter requires more mind bending than a trip on LSD.

People join the Society on the premise that Welch wants to win the shooting match against Communism in Vietnam. Once they've signed the dotted line, however, it eventually becomes necessary for the Society to be more explicit. The Society's Vietnam nightmare requires Birch rookies to have a childlike faith in the infallibility of Robert Welch, endless patience in working their way out of a maze of startling revelations and a keen sense of humor.

The Birch story on the Big Muddy begins in earnest in 1954, when Welch says our U.S. government went to the Geneva Conference to throw the French out of Vietnam and put the Communists in. "Communists could just as easily have had all of Vietnam handed to them instead of merely North Vietnam," Welch says. Our observers set it up this way so that a war could be arranged between North and South Vietnam at a later date. You know, two hands of one body, etc.

Welch explains this American treason in a Birch pamphlet entitled, oddly enough, *The Truth In Time*: "As so-called 'observers' at Geneva in 1954, but really running the show, we turned the top half of the country over directly and officially to the Communists, and set up an anti-Communist government in the bottom half, exactly as we had done in Korea in 1948. In both cases we thus prepared the way for the Communist aggression from the northern part into the southern part, and for the war that would follow, exactly as the Communists were already planning."

At this point, the greenhorn Bircher is usually blinking in perplexity and looking heavenwards for assistance in understanding step one in the Welchian history of Southeast Asia. If he is brazen enough to question this Birch revelation, it may be necessary to detour to the Korean War momentarily and overwhelm the rookie with enough Welchian logic to convince him that his is not to question why, but to do and die for the sake of all our children, our children's children and untold generations of children to come.

142

Reassured that he is on the right track toward smashing the Insider conspiracy, it is time to move on. The next delicate maneuver, as Welch sees it, was to install Ngo Dinh Diem as Prime Minister of Vietnam in 1954, and then as President in 1955. The master story teller told it like it is, Birch style, in the August, 1966 *Bulletin:* "For the past two or three years we have been trying hard to tell our members, and anybody else who would listen, that the Ngo Dinh Diem regime in South Vietnam had been used by the Eisenhower and Kennedy administrations to destroy all effective anti-Communist forces in South Vietnam."

"Hold it there a minute!" shouts the new Bircher excitedly. "Every conservative report I've ever read said that Diem was a paragon of virtue and the greatest anti-Communist in Vietnam."

True enough. Almost every other conservative leader in the country backed the Diem regime to the hilt. Some of them knew Diem, Nhu or Madame Nhu personally. All attested to the anti-Communism of the Ngo family. They have been stunned, shocked and outraged by the Welch line. The battle over Diem, his brother, Ngo Dinh Nhu, and the beautiful Madame Nhu (who served as official first lady for her brother-in-law), was a vicious one. Welch painted the entire Ngo family as pro-Communist. He asserted that Nhu and his wife were more powerful than Diem, and that these two were actual leaders of the Communists.

The sputtering Bircher is obviously confused by all this conflicting testimony. The easiest way to overcome doubt is to seek the written words of Prophet Welch in one of his inevitable pamphlets—this time one appropriately

143

titled *Wild Statements*. "All effective anti-Communist resistance in South Vietnam had been destroyed or completely demoralized by the end of the Eisenhower Administration. So much so that when the time was
approaching to put on the show we are now engaged in,
of helping the South Vietnamese to save their country
from Communism, the Ngo Dinh Diem crowd simply had
to be eliminated. . . . The Ngo family was so utterly
discredited as anti-Communists, in the minds of all South
Vietnamese, that it could no longer even pose in that
capacity. So, having served their purpose for the Communists, they were now expendable."

At this point Welch says the "fiction" that Diem was an
anti-Communist had to be preserved among conservatives. Welch maintains that the conspiracy, therefore,
selected a French anti-Communist, Suzanne Labin, as
the primary promoter of the theme that Diem and his
family had to be saved. Then, when Diem and his
brother, Ngo Dinh Nhu, were toppled from power and
assassinated in 1963, all Diem's American conservative
supporters jumped on Miss Labin's bandwagon according
to plan and were tricked into supporting Presidents Kennedy and Johnson in the name of anti-Communism.

"But the very next step in this same propaganda line,"
Welch says, "is that we must now fight the Viet Cong,
and even the Red Chinese, if necessary, to protect and
continue these anti-Communist gains—and must do so
under the direction and control of Henry Cabot Lodge.
There has never been a more frightening exposition of
Communist confidence in the short memories, ignorance,
indifference, and gullibility of the American people!"

Speaking of gullibility, it is necessary to know where

Robert Welch gets his information. Welch's chief, and perhaps only, source of information regarding Vietnam is Hilaire du Berrier, long-time French correspondent for *American Opinion*. Welch says that there are few men anywhere in the world as well equipped with firsthand knowledge and on-the-spot experience as du Berrier.

Hilaire du Berrier, an American born adventurer, began his unusual career barnstorming with a flying circus at the age of 20. When the Spanish Civil War began, du Berrier joined the Loyalist Forces as a pursuit pilot; that is, he was on the same side as the Communists.

As du Berrier tells the story, the Communists then received reports from Paris that du Berrier was an anti-Communist and quickly arrested him. He was released through the efforts of Colonel Alberto Bayo, who was one of the organizers of the revolt which overthrew the Spanish monarchy in the first place. Bayo later fled Spain and became a Mexican citizen. Du Berrier says he was helped by Bayo because the loyalists didn't want to offend Eleanor Roosevelt by executing an American citizen.

Next, du Berrier, by now a confirmed soldier of fortune, sailed to the Orient in anticipation of another war. He became involved in intrigue for Chiang Kai-shek agents and French resistance forces before being jailed by the Japanese for three years.

Following this, Du Berrier went to work for the Office of Strategic Services, and later for *Newsweek* magazine. He has said that he lost both jobs because of opposition to U.S. support of Ho Chi Minh.

His career is sketchy for the next ten years, but du Berrier eventually became very much opposed to the Diem government after supporting it earlier. The rumor

145

circulated that du Berrier was dropped by Diem and became revengeful. Du Berrier denies this.

The Birch Society's Western Islands publishing house began distributing du Berrier's book on Vietnam, *Background to Betrayal,* in 1965. Welch calls it the most comprehensive book published in English on the matter of the U.S. government-Communist plot to create chaos in Vietnam "ever since we put Ho Chi Minh in business with our money and equipment in 1944."

In his book du Berrier lays the chief responsibility for our mess in Vietnam on a close working alliance between the Central Intelligence Agency and professors at Michigan State University. The CIA, he maintains, spent a fortune building the image of the Diem regime in the U.S. Du Berrier says the regime promoted Communism, rather than fighting it. Once again, the Birch Society has strange bedfellows; it is the extreme left-wing in America which most consistently attacks the CIA, especially CIA activities on college campuses.

Rookie Birchers, if they are able to decipher this double-think, are usually appalled to discover that Welch does not share the usual conservative support of our government's decision to fight the Communists in Vietnam. Consistent with his recurrent theme that the U.S. government is Communist controlled, Welch advises that Birchers condemn the stands of the last three administrations—which seems to put a Bircher in the same position as the Hippies, Yippies and Dr. Spock. In as much as this alignment comes as natural to a Bircher as a fish taking to a tree house, it is hopeless to inspire fidelity among the few members who occasionally think for themselves. Those who are just too numb to think at all are liable to throw in the sponge completely and ask, "How about if I forget about Vietnam and just worry about impeaching the Supreme Court?"

Parents of servicemen who are killed in action sometimes gravitate to the Birch Society in the purest grief over the Vietnam dilemma. Disillusioned and angered by what appears to be a wasteful "no-win" strategy, they join the Society with the patriotic intention of backing all the boys in Vietnam. It is almost inconceivable to think that these people who want the consolation that their sons' deaths contributed to a great cause could ever accept the Birch line that they died in vain, mere victims of a gruesome charade acted out for the devious designs of the Insiders.

There are a number of assumptions which each member of the Birch Society must swallow before he can actively promote the Birch position on Vietnam. They are as follows:

(1) *The Communists have working control of our government.*

(2) *The Vietnam War is being waged by Washington as a method of helping Communism.* This is a logical extension of the first premise.

(3) *The U.S. government deliberately installed the Communist regime in North Vietnam and completely contrived the Vietnam war.*

(4) *The Russia-China rift is a Communist fraud.*

(5) *The Insiders don't want us to get out of Vietnam;* they want us to stay and fight. This assumption requires some explanation. The Insiders, says Welch, are using their exact reversal tactic to make us think that they

147

want us to withdraw from South Vietnam. But they don't really care about Vietnam. They just want us to fight over it. In Welch's words: "So the problem of how thus to get and keep the United States involved in Vietnam had, for the Communists, a very simple solution. All they needed was merely to have a few thousand of their agents and dupes and stooges stage some parades and establish some picket lines, *protesting* our being in Vietnam, and demanding that we withdraw. And at once, with the help of high ranking propagandists who are *not* recognized as pro-Communist, the American people become convinced that the Communists do not want us fighting in Vietnam; and that therefore we *must* support the Administration in doing so."*

Get that, conservatives? Next time you pass a group of beatniks protesting the war, foil 'em! Join them, and help fight Communism by demanding that we pull out of Vietnam!

(6) *The Vietnam war is being run by the UN.* This seems to conflict with the second assumption. However, when you remember that Washington and Moscow are merely puppets, or Communist fronts, for the Insiders, this apparent contradiction is relatively unimportant. The point is, according to Welch, the war in Vietnam is being run on the basis of SEATO treaties, and is ultimately under the control of the United Nations.

Even Robert Welch felt he had to explain this incredible conclusion. He says that the administration, or the Communists or the Insiders (whichever you prefer) knew that the American people wouldn't stand for an-

* *A Touch of Sanity,* by Robert Welch, in pamphlet form and on film.

other United Nations war like Korea, so they slid into Vietnam on the basis of SEATO commitments. Welch "proves" that this SEATO war in Vietnam is actually a United Nations war in Vietnam, by merely quoting two articles from the United Nations Charter—as if anybody ever paid much attention to the United Nations Charter.

Quotations from the pertinent articles are:

Chapter I., Article 2. The parties undertake, as set forth in the Charter of the United Nations . . . "to refrain in their international relations from the threat or use of force . . . in any manner inconsistent with the purposes of the United Nations."

Chapter VII., Article 51. Each party . . . agrees that it will . . . act to meet the common danger in accordance with its constitutional processes. *"Measures taken [under this paragraph] shall be immediately reported to the Security Council [of the United Nations]* . . ." (Welch's emphasis)

Assuming that our government did consider the Vietnam war to be a SEATO war, and assuming that they did report to the Security Council—so what? A report to the Security Council, whether a blunt announcement that we're in Vietnam or a lengthy dissertation about what we're trying to do there, hardly constitutes United Nations control over the war or our way of conducting it.

As if to scare everyone silly, Welch also points out ominously that the required reporting is supposed to be made to the Undersecretary of the United Nations for Political and Security Affairs and that this office has always been filled by a Communist. At no time, however, does he offer any information that we're actually filing reports with the United Nations, or that if we are, the reports contain any inside information that would be useful to the enemy. Besides, why worry about it? If the Insiders are running both Moscow and Washington, they hardly need United Nations reports to be kept informed of their own subversive activity.

The inconsistencies, implications, and fantasies are so hopelessly unbelievable, illogical and morally reprehensible that it's almost impossible to understand how one man could have worked all this out and foisted it upon the gullible members of the John Birch Society in the name of anti-Communism. As I write this, I am amazed that it took me so long to awake from this utterly ridiculous phantasmagoria of nonsense. P. T. Barnum seems a piker by comparison.

Fortunately, Welch's abilities as a persuader haven't been matched by his ability to make predictions. He sees the following results from the war in Vietnam:

(1) *Red China will enter the war.* Welch predicted this in 1965. Later he explained that the Red Chinese have a hundred million surplus men they want to get rid of. This is the same line taken by the doves who insist that escalation will bring us into direct conflict with Red China. Welch's position on this point does not exactly support the right-wing demand for a quick and decisive victory in Vietnam. The leader of the John Birch Society seems to be propagandizing against one of his own slogans, Victory, Then Peace.

(2) *We're fighting in Vietnam simply to be at war.* This is Welch's conclusion about why we're in Vietnam. The idea is expressed in Shakespeare's line, "Be it thy course to busy giddy minds with foreign quarrels." By focusing American attention on Vietnam, Welch reasons,

the Communists can more easily continue their internal subversion in America.

(3) *The war in Vietnam gives Washington an excuse to fasten wartime controls over the American people.* Welch predicted that we would have rationing several years ago. When this failed to happen, he said the election had changed the situation. Welch is now prophesying more taxes, more agencies and more government paternalism—certainly a safe bet in view of the history of America for the last forty years. This increased government control will soon result in a Communist police state, Welch says. It is interesting that the New Left also predicts we will soon have a police state—a fascist one in their estimation.

(4) *The U.S. will be merged into a Communist world government.* Welch predicts that as we pour more and more troops into Vietnam to fight the Red Chinese, Russia will pretend to be our ally. The Soviet Union will then step forward as a mediator and arrange for everybody, including themselves, to come together peacefully under the United Nations. This, Welch says, would turn out to be a one-world Communist government.

Robert Welch and the John Birch Society have proposed solutions for the mess in Vietnam. Welch says we ought to:

(1) Stop trading with Russia, China and other Communist nations that are supplying North Vietnam.

(2) Let the U.S. military win the war quickly and decisively.

(3) Set up a firm anti-Communist government in Saigon.

151

(4) Issue a strong ultimatum to Hanoi and Peking to stay out of South Vietnam.

(5) Bring our troops home.

Now let us examine what the Birch Society is doing to persuade our government to accomplish these goals. The Birch program is two-pronged: education and action.

The educational aspect consists of persuading Society members to distribute copies of Birch publications which explain the Vietnam situation as Welch sees it.

Birchers participate in the action phase of the program in a number of ways. First, they are urged to write a slew of letters each week to Senators, Congressmen, editors, broadcasters and other opinion molders to promote the Birch goals for Vietnam. They are reminded to use the Society's slogans for this project:

When are we going to win this war in Vietnam—and why not?

Why fight 'em in Vietnam and help 'em everywhere else?

Victory, Then Peace.

The third slogan was reportedly put into service when it was discovered that the first two were far too long to put on a bumper strip. It was also needed to help counteract the impression that the Birch Society wanted to pull out of Vietnam, which was created by another slogan, "Get US Out" (referring to the UN), and by Welch himself. He did, in fact, hint at this once or twice, but was so chastised by some Birchers and other conservatives that he revised his approach and made it clear that we should only get out of Vietnam after winning a military victory.

Birchers also form front organizations called TRAIN

(To Restore American Independence Now) Committees. The Society has had paid staffmen travelling throughout the country devoting full time to just setting up these committees. The TRAIN steering committees are composed solely of Birchers, but the stated goal is to enlist "as many non-Birchers as possible in these activities." A series of manuals is available to direct the step-by-step development of these committees into efficient and powerful Birch fronts.

The prescribed TRAIN activities include: writing hundreds of letters each month through workshops, securing signatures on petitions, organizing study programs, forming speakers bureaus and holding Victory in Vietnam rallies.

The major thrust of the Birch war on Vietnam is petitions to Congress. The Society claims to have secured one-and-a-half million unduplicated signatures on petitions displayed at such places as doctors' offices, barber shops and filling stations.

The object of the petition crusade is to pressure Washington officials to curb trade with Communist countries dealing with North Vietnam. You would expect that in order to exert maximum influence, Society officials would give the petitions to those Senators and Representatives who are wavering in their opinions. Not so. Almost all have been submitted to hawks who are already fully committed on the issue. For this reason, the campaign has been a total waste to the conservative movement. But Welch admitted in a *Bulletin* that a by-product of the petition drive "can be its aid to recruitment." As a former staff member of the Society, I suspect this has been the primary motive all along.

153

Robert Welch opened both his speech and pamphlet entitled *The Truth About Vietnam* by quoting the lead sentence of an editorial which appeared in the Boston *Herald* on January 21, 1967: "Last week in Vietnam 144 Americans were killed, 1,004 were wounded and six were reported missing." He then asked an intentionally shocking question. He asked if this constituted "deliberate, conscious, and cold-blooded murder" on the part of the Johnson Administration.

This technique was reminiscent of a statement about the Korean Reds made by the famed expert on brainwashing and propaganda, Edward Hunter, to a Congressional Committee in 1958.

"The Red indoctrinators built up this impression and fit it into their pattern of selfish, imperialistic America led by bloated Wall Street financiers who were using our people as cannon fodder."*

Is Robert Welch doing the same thing with his Insider concept?

* *Communist Psychological Warfare,* consultation with Edward Hunter, Committee on Un-American Activities, p. 16, March 13, 1958.

13

Bipartisan Treason

Robert Welch has been busy over the years denying the charge that his ultimate motives are political. He says that the Society is not a political organization and that he seeks no power over anyone at anytime. Certainly it could be argued that Birchers do not practice the finer points of politics, which has been defined as the art of human happiness. I can't recall Birchers ever making anybody happy—except, perhaps, Art Buchwald who has gotten a lot of mileage out of poking fun at them. On the other hand, Henry Adams once said that practical politics consists in ignoring facts. Birchers excel at this.

The Birch Society is incorporated in Massachusetts as an educational organization. It has never publicly endorsed a political candidate, given financial assistance to a political party, or told its members how to vote. The

Society is strictly bi-partisan, accusing both Republicans and Democrats of treason.

At times the Society has been shell-shocked by serious splits within the membership over which candidates to support. In 1966 there was nearly a second civil war in Georgia when Birchers clashed over the Bo Calloway-Lester Mattox gubernatorial race. In 1968 Birchers all over the nation divided between Nixon and Reagan for the Republican nomination, and then between Nixon and Wallace in the grand finale.

Despite numerous statements by Welch and other Birch officials about the Society's complete aloofness from the political arena, suspicions still linger that the John Birch Society is essentially a political organization which ultimately seeks control over the United States. In part, this fear is caused by the fact that the Society's greatest growth and most intense activity take place during major political campaigns. This is natural. They'd be crazy not to capitalize on political opportunities as a means of recruiting new members.

A large percentage of the Society's members are very active in local politics. This was especially evident during the 1964 Republican National Convention where 100 delegates and alternates were Birchers for Goldwater.

The Birch Society also evokes fanatical reaction from politicians who resent known Birchers working energetically for their opponents. On the other hand, many liberal politicians have found the Birch Society to be a wonderful stigma with which to brand a more conservative opponent.

The Society sometimes becomes a political football and is kicked back and forth unmercifully. The liberal

156

accuses the conservative of being a "Birchist," an "extremist," or an "ultra-rightist." The conservative, alarmed at being skewered and roasted as an irresponsible fascist, strikes back by citing his family's war record against the Nazis and denouncing the Society even more than his liberal opponent. Politicians can always shake hands after the campaign, but the Birch Society is a loser every election day.

Welch made one of his typical blunders when he gave a major speech at a 1965 rally held in Chicago by Kent Courtney's Conservative Society of America. The convention of conservatives had been called to form a new national third party. Welch's appearance was interpreted as a sign that he endorsed a third party movement. This was a natural conclusion, but Welch was peeved that everyone took it that way.

A few months later the Society opened a branch office just a few blocks from the White House, and it looked like Birchers were working hard to influence Congress. Reed Benson, who headed the office, registered as a lobbyist and made national headlines the first day by telling newsmen that President Johnson's policy on trade with Communist nations "falls under the category of treason." Reed Benson also referred to the Eisenhower administration as "basically a tragic page in history." This was ironic as his father, Ezra Taft Benson, helped write that "tragic page" for eight years as Eisenhower's Secretary of Agriculture.

During the last few years Welch has been flirting with the idea of taking a much more direct interest in influencing elections. A pilot program to test this idea was organized in California, the greatest source of Birch strength. Birchers claimed credit for the election of Ronald Reagan—much to the consternation of the Governor. Birch boasting in California was silenced in 1968, however, when long-time Birch-baiter Alan Cranston defeated Max Rafferty, the staunch conservative hero, for the U.S. Senate.

The Society has a secret, grass-roots, quasi-political program called Project Knowledge which a special, private Birch manual describes this way: "This network uses the precinct organizational structure, not for political action per se, but as a readily available, understandable-by-all, tool for spreading knowledge. The total overall aim of the program is to reach the goal set by Mr. Welch —that of obtaining 1,000 members in each Congressional district. . . ."

Based on results achieved in their California experiment, the Society says that it knows how to "guarantee a permanent vote" for just 15 cents—which would compare fantastically well with the usual political expenditure of 50 cents to 60 cents per vote for one election.

Consequently, Welch has decided to expand Project Knowledge into other states as fast as the money can be raised to do it properly. He wants $20 million in order to build 50 Birch chapters in each of 325 Congressional districts (three-fourths of the 435 Congressional districts in the nation). Every chapter would have approximately 20 members—giving a total of "1,000 ideological salesmen" in each district.

This strength, Welch says, could "exercise enough influence over political thinking within that district to control the political action there." The money has not been forthcoming; but if it suddenly materialized Welch would concentrate his "quasi-political" activities in the low-population Western states where it would be easiest and least expensive to build conservative strength in the U.S. Senate.*

The Society also uses its usual petition campaigns and letter-writing crusades to influence politicians already in Congress. Welch introduced an assortment of books and pamphlets called the "Packet for Politicians" in July, 1966. Members were urged to buy packets for $2.95 and send them gratis to local office-holders in order to alert them, Birch style, to the dangers of Communism. It didn't go over too well. Most conservative Birchers don't feel a politician is worth $2.95. Birchers acquire this attitude from Robert Welch who has heaped scorn on the "venal" politicians on many occasions.

Welch's urge to get into the political arena as a king-maker led him to secretly organize a new movement, called "The 1976 Committee" in the spring of 1966. The name of Robert Welch does not appear as an officer or sponsor of this new organization, although people closely associated with the Society know he was the guiding light behind it. William J. Grede, chairman of the Executive Committee of the Council of the John Birch Society, is also chairman of The 1976 Committee. Its list of officers and sponsors is loaded with other Birch Council members.

The 1976 Committee is supposed to accomplish its goal of restoring the American Constitutional Republic and go out of business by July 4, 1976, the 200th anni-

* These low-population states elect two Senators, the same as high-population states such as New York and Pennsylvania where the job would be infinitely more difficult and costly.

versary of our American Republic. The Committee was set up for the purpose of nominating Ezra Taft Benson as president and Senator Strom Thurmond as vice president.

Printed materials on how they're going to bring this about are contradictory. One brochure proposes that conservatives work toward making these two men the candidates of both the Republican and Democratic parties. Bipartisan treason then becomes Birch all-Americanism. Another piece recommends that this be done "within the framework of the Republican Party as we feel this party is more conservative than is the Democrat Party."

Birch politics are not the politics of joy. Birchers sometimes resort to "dirty pool" during elections. In southern Florida there is no liberal hated more by Birchers than Congressman Claude Pepper from Miami. They've nicknamed him "Red" Pepper.

During the 1962 campaign Pepper ran for re-election. He used signs which said "Support JFK—Pull Lever 1A." The night before the election, two Birchers were caught by Miami police while distributing illegal posters in Negro neighborhoods. The posters said "Support JFK—Pull Lever 7A." One of these men also printed illegal "Pinko Pepper" literature and had it distributed in violation of a legal cut-off date for new election literature.

The other Bircher pulled another gigantic boner two years later when Pepper ran for re-election against conservative Paul O'Neill. He told O'Neill's wife that the only mistake Adolf Hitler made was that he did not make the ovens big enough to kill all the Jews. Mrs. O'Neill is Jewish.

Birch headquarters in Belmont was informed of the

160

antics of these two men and it was recommended that they be booted out of the Society. The Birch Society would not revoke their memberships.

Political campaigns are exciting times around the Birch Society. Most Birchers are intensely interested in partisan politics and practically every campaign results in titanic struggles between individual Birchers who don't see eye to eye on which politicians to support.

As a professional Bircher, it was difficult to keep from being drawn into these political bloodlettings. I particularly remember one heated campaign. A well-known Birch candidate for the Florida State Legislature publicly called another conservative politician who was running for Congress the vilest right-wing epitaph imaginable: "a planted agent of C.O.P.E." (the AFL-CIO's Committee on Political Education). As GOP County Chairman this Congressional candidate had risked his future many times to defend Birchers on the County Executive Committee. For this reason, the charge, accompanied by an endorsement of the man's opponent, brought on a gigantic battle. My telephone rang incessantly as each side insisted that I renounce the other. I packed my bags and quickly left town for a week until the election was over.

Another candidate accused me of deliberately trying to sabotage his campaign. I had never met this man and was not even aware that he was running for office. When I angrily called his office and demanded an explanation for his statements, he blandly reasoned that since I was not traveling about the countryside actively rounding up supporters and funds for him, I must be an enemy. "He who is not for me is against me." Welchian logic.

At the same time still another Birch member was running for the State Senate against an encumbent, solely on the strength of having a last name that would appear first on the ballot. This was his entire campaign strategy. He did not give speeches or spend money. He damn near won, too.

14

When in Doubt,
Form a Committee

Birchers are not the bravest people in the world. Most of them are secretive about their membership. Many of them prefer to use pseudonyms when signing Birch letters. And when Birchers have a special project to promote, they generally form an innocuous-sounding front organization to preserve their Birch anonymity and respectability.

This has led to a rash (some would call it a plague) of Birch front organizations to embrace every conceivable Birch activity. The Birch Society has published comprehensive manuals instructing members on even the most minute details of how to set up and finance a front committee. However, the Birch Society does not call them "front committees," a name which connotes the Communists who have used them to great advantage.

Rather, Birchers call their front groups "ad hoc committees" and are quick to explain in their manuals that "ad hoc committees have long been a custom in America and are a time-honored method of free people banding together to promote, educate, and petition for specific programs."

Time-honored Birch front groups also serve the very important purpose of roping non-Birchers into their corral—people who otherwise would not be caught dead serving Birch purposes. Theoretically, all sponsors and endorsers of an ad hoc committee are supposed to be informed of the connection with the Birch Society. Theoretically, that is. Birchers quite often forget about this little detail in their enthusiasm to rub elbows with respected citizens.

I once attended a TRAIN Committee meeting that was organized to discredit the United Nations. In a few minutes it was quite obvious to me that the Birchers I recognized in the room were hiding the fact that the committee had any connection with the Society. They were prattling innocently about how awful it was that the United Nations was sometimes given more press play than our own Congress, and that this could lead to some sort of world government that would do us all in.

When I steered the discussion into deeper channels about the Communist conspiracy and the Birch program, it was apparent that the non-Birchers were becoming restless and the Birchers were practically going into shock. Naturally, someone got around to asking me about my connection with the committee. I answered nonchalantly, "I'm the state coordinator for the John Birch Society." Three clergymen and two prominent business ex-

164

ecutives paled considerably, and all five found reasons to depart before our business was half over.

Inducing notable people to sponsor Birch ad hoc committees is a carefully formulated part of the Society's manual for TRAIN Committees. The program is so meticulously laid out that one whole section is devoted to specifying the precise language to use when telephoning people to ask them to serve. Possible embarrassing questions are enumerated, along with the proper answers to overcome resistance. The questions in the manual are asked by "Harry Hostile," and "A. Bill Leader" answers them competently from the Birch viewpoint.

Support Your Local Police Committees have been the most popular and most successful Birch fronts. After wallowing in the controversial quagmires of impeaching Earl Warren and undermining the civil rights movement, and ranting about UNICEF and other United Nations programs, Birchers took the police to their bosoms like a little girl embraces her first dolly.

Like anyone else, Birchers love to be loved, and with the program of supporting the local guardians of law and order, how could they go wrong? They took off on the project like a motorcycle cop chasing a speeder. Hundreds of thousands of bumpers suddenly sported "Support Your Local Police" strips (the fact that they were known to help ward off traffic tickets from sympathetic policemen helped some). Billboards proclaimed the same all over America. Schools held essay contests. Radio stations ran special promotion spots. Mayors throughout the nation proclaimed Support Your Local Police Week. The publicity was so great that the firemen got jealous. They put out their own bumper strips, "Support Your Local Fire Fighters." It was the Birch Society's finest hour.

The latest Birch front is called MOTOREDE (Movement to Restore Decency). Its purpose is to offer organized, nationwide and determined opposition to sex-education programs in public schools. Welch calls these sex-education courses "subversive monstrosities" and a "filthy Communist plot."

Conservatives are angry about the Birch campaign against sex-education courses. Many non-Birchers have legitimate reservations and complaints about this program. They are reluctant to bring them out in the open, however, for fear they will be accused of being Birchers. Once again, by using the Communist label to smear the opposition, the Birchers have defeated their own purpose.

The most controversial ad hoc committee is TACT (Truth About Civil Turmoil). TACT committees are organized to support Welch's contention that "the movement known as 'civil rights' is Communist-plotted, Communist-controlled, and in fact . . . serves only Communist purposes." Initiated in 1965, TACT groups have multiplied all over the nation. They sponsor speakers, buy newspaper ads, distribute pamphlets and pepper Congressmen and newspaper editors with propaganda exposing the "truth about civil turmoil."

The primary TACT Committee weapons are the before-mentioned anti-civil rights book called *It's Very Simple,* written for the Society by Alan Stang; a filmstrip, "Show Biz In the Streets"; and a one-hour and fifteen-minute film, "Anarchy U.S.A."

Civil Rights Seminars were another vital Birch bludg-

166

eon against the civil rights movement. This extensive program was not announced publicly in the *Bulletin,* but sprang up suddenly in selected localities before opposition could form. In special printed instructions, sponsors were advised to "choose a front name such as 'Parents for Racial Harmony' or 'Citizens for Understanding Civil Rights' or 'Committee for Better Understanding.'"

Step two was to "head the committee with a respected and well known person, whose character is unassailable. . . . Try to gain the support of the American Legion and the Veterans of Foreign Wars. . . . In other words, draw as much community support as possible." Next they had to cough up approximately $2,000 for a complete package which included: seven speakers, 10,000 flyers, fifty window posters, taped radio spots, TV ads, billboard posters, newspaper ads, news releases and sample solicitation letters to merchants, church groups, and fraternal and civic organizations.

The sample "profit-sharing ticket sales" letter to businessmen said in part, "No doubt you have noticed that there is a great deal of confusion—and consequent controversy—in our city about the matter of 'Civil Rights.' Most everyone has something to say about this issue, but how many of us really *know* the whole story?" After brief information about the seminar, the letter continues, "You need have no fear that such a program may be 'inflamatory' or escalate a problem. On the contrary, we feel that *mutual understanding* is the key to the solution."

Our mutual understanding program included the new film, "Anarchy U.S.A.," which was expertly designed to "prove" that the civil rights turmoil now tormenting this country follows the same pattern and purposes of similar revolutions carried out by Communists in China, Cuba and Algeria.

The "Anarchy" film has been shown everywhere in America with far-reaching results. Several hundred prints are in use continually, sometimes before audiences of many hundreds of attentive Americans. Police forces have been singled out for special previews and they have been most cooperative in spreading its impact to other citizens.

I showed this film many times myself, sometimes even going into ghetto areas for presentations before exclusively Negro groups. This was a bit risky and unTACTful perhaps in light of the fact that "Anarchy" makes the following accusations:

1. President John F. Kennedy gave "aid and comfort to the enemy that means to conquer the world" when he cooperated with Algeria's Ben Bella.

2. "We Shall Overcome" and "Freedom Now" are Communist slogans.

3. Assassinated hero Medgar Evers "helped promote Communist agitation."

4. The Civil Rights Act of 1964 was a "vicious legislative step on the road to tyranny."

5. The Voting Rights Bill of 1965 was another step toward tyranny.

6. The civil rights movement is part of a worldwide Communist conspiracy.

As if this wasn't bad enough, the Birch film mocks Martin Luther King when he is shown denying Communist involvement, shows a Florida racist screaming that

"LBJ is the biggest nigger-lover in the U.S.A.," and dwells on Ku Klux Klan and National States Rights Party spokesmen berating "Martin Lucifer Coon" and race-mixing mongrelization.

I must have been out of my mind when I took this film to groups of Negroes on their own stamping grounds. I fully realized the danger. Expecting the tires to be slashed without fail, I took the mercenary precaution of using my wife's battered 1955 Oldsmobile instead of my new VW bus.

The effect of the film was stunning. Bug-eyed, unblinking, and immobile for the entire showing, these people were too shocked at the film to respond with anything but amazement. Perhaps they had pity on me, thinking I must be mentally deranged to show up alone in their neighborhood with a film like that.

Believe it or not, I was gullible and sincere enough to hope that I could save Negroes from what I considered a Communist plot by exposing them to the proper Birch materials. That I came out of it alive is a tribute to Negro patience, tolerance and compassion.

In the end, it was their attitude that converted me, not vice versa. Whenever I heard someone complain about the "niggers" and how we ought to ship them back to Africa—and perhaps sink the ships on the way—I thought of two black men who live in Sarasota. One man, a school teacher, had his home bombed twice and a new car burned beyond recovery because he believes in law and order and refused to cooperate with a group of hot-head agitators.

The other man—who built a beautiful home for his family with his own two hands when local banks

169

wouldn't loan him money because he was a Negro—
nearly lost his daughter when his house was set afire by
some black goons. He had refused to join a gang of
radicals bent on violence and had dared to report their
plans to the police because he was a good citizen. I
decided I wouldn't want to trade these two courageous
Americans for a hundred whites wearing "Never!" but-
tons and sending out mimeographed, anonymous hate
literature through the mail.

15

Coming to Grips
With Myself

It was a Negro—a muscular, intense, illiterate sanitation department worker—who finally set me straight about the absurdities I was suckling from the Birch Society and spitting up on society in general. He weaned me forcefully, almost violently, from the security of the simplistic answers of the Birch Society, and introduced me to the realities of a complex world in turmoil.

It happened on one of my insane trips into a ghetto with "Anarchy U.S.A." It was a Saturday night and I, at the urging of a middle-class, black businessman who for some unknown reason thought that the Birch Society had something to offer him, was appearing at a decrepit Negro church.

The audience was predictably bad that night, with no more than a handful of black people appearing to see a free film by an organization which most of them had never heard of. The old, gnarled black pastor *had* heard of the Birch Society. He sat in the back of his church, stonefaced and sorry, but willing to endure the evening to accommodate the black businessman who was obviously one of the few affluent members in the congregation.

The sanitation worker watched the film in silent horror, as did the other spectators. When it was over, he sputtered in rage, finding adequate words hard to come by. We locked in chin to chin verbal combat before he was able to vent the full steam of his emotions in language I could understand.

"You come here with talk about free enterprise and property rights and how the Communists are gonna take it all away and how all the rioting and looting is gonna lead to a new civil war and lots of people are gonna get hurt. Man, let me tell you something. I ain't had nothin' all my life and now for the first time I'm beginnin' to get *something* and it's *because* of all the rioting and looting because none of you charlies ever paid no attention before. And let me tell you this, you sitting pretty in your nice neighborhood in your nice home with your nice children and your nice lawn. One of these day we's coming down your street in our dirty clothes and our new cars you whiteys get rich collecting on and we's gonna get a piece of the action. And if you don't give it to us, we's gonna take it."

I squinted my eyes at this, set my chin, pointed my finger into his chest and answered back through clenched teeth, "You do that. And if you try, just remember one thing. If you come down my street and threaten the security of my home, I'll put a bullet right between your eyes."

This brought a surprising roar of laughter from my adversary. When the laughter faded, he gritted his teeth once more and became stunningly cooperative and practical.

"OK, white boy. You say we gotta worry about the Communists. You say they using us. You say this whole thing gonna lead to slavery. What the hell you think we got now, white boy? I ain't got no education. Weren't no need to get one. Couldn't do anything with it anyway. I ain't got a decent place to live. Landlord won't fix it up and I won't do it for him. Can't move because whitey won't let us out of our side of town. Can't live here no more 'cause I can't stand it any more. Things are bad for me. Always been bad. But they used to be worse. Before the rioting and looting you keep screaming about, I couldn't even get a job. I couldn't sit in one of your restaurants—even if I had money enough to. I couldn't ride in front of a bus. Couldn't even walk on the streets outside my own neighborhood. Cop would stop me and ask me what I'm up to. Yes, things are a little better now and they're better 'cause some of us black people ain't playing dead for whitey anymore. Yes, things are getting better because we're scaring hell out of whitey. OK—now you say the Communists are using us. Civil rights are a trick. The government's making slaves of us. If all that's true, *you* tell me how else I gonna get someplace? How else I gonna get a better job? How else I gonna walk anywhere I want and the cops let me alone? C'mon, white boy, tell us how we do it your way?"

The question stopped me completely. Time, capitalism, pull yourself up by your bootstraps, work hard to get ahead, clean up your neighborhood, be creative—all these things seem stupid when you're starting into the desperate eyes of a man who's deprived and angry and determined. I didn't say anything. I couldn't. Everything I was doing was suddenly very stupid. My slogans, my films, my well prepared answers, my books—all were very stupid and so very, very inadequate. Suddenly, for the first time, I was ashamed.

I was brought back to my senses that night in that rundown, Negro church. The truth confronted me in the form of a crude, rude, angry garbageman. It was a most unlikely source; but then, doesn't truth always seem to come from the most unlikely people at the most unlikely times? Thank God I was still open to the truth because my motivations, although foolish, had been somewhat pure. I wasn't in the Birch Society primarily for money. I hadn't been completely dulled to absurdity and irrationality.

I still hated intolerance, bigotry and hypocrisy wherever and whenever I found them—even within my own organization. As Tennessee Williams said when he converted to Catholicism, "I wanted my goodness back." That Negro sanitation worker helped me find my goodness again.

But the tense confrontation with the Negro man was only the immediate cause of my conversion. There had been many other disturbing things welling up inside my mind for some time. Ever since I spent time with Robert Welch I had serious doubts about the foundations for all his basic premises which Birchers are asked to take for granted. It began to occur to me that the generalizations

I blindly accepted from Welch were far more fantastic than the generalizations I was totally unwilling to accept from my own elected government. With the government, at least I could hope to help make some changes through use of the ballot box. With the Birch Society, I was stuck with whatever theory Welch decided to propagate as the policy of the entire organization.

Also, the very things that had made mundane, medio-cre middle-class American life so repulsive began to seem a mite more attractive. I had wanted a measure of fame. The Birch Society gave me this in the form of notoriety. In time, however, this novelty wore off and it was not especially pleasurable to be sought after for the kooki-ness of right-wing views rather than for the merit of my own opinions.

I even became disillusioned with what I supposedly was fighting for through the auspices of the John Birch Society. Robert Welch is first and foremost a business-man—a Babbitt, if you please. He founded the Birch Society around typical chamber-of-commerce-type busi-nessmen and he ran the Society like it was a giant corpo-ration. Working for the Society brought me into contact with the kind of men Welch personified. To me they seemed a relatively unprincipled lot—empty of dedica-tion, self-sacrifice, compassion or even self-respect. For the most part, they were cynical, self-serving and superfi-cial. While Welch seemed to accept men such as these as the "soul" of the American free-enterprise system (which to some approaches the status of a religion), I was un-willing to believe they represented the best the American way had to offer.

I first took up Birchism as a cause with the false

175

impression that it was an extension of my own religious beliefs—a holy crusade against the insidious advances of atheistic Communism.

Nothing could have been further from the truth. Birchism is entirely removed from the charity, humility and sincere quest for justice that characterized the life of Christ. Bombing the hell out of every nation that doesn't agree with us hardly seems consistent with the Christian ideal of turning the other cheek. Contemptuously rejecting the Negro, Mexican-American and Indian civil rights movements as Communist conspiracies without offering any workable alternatives to solve the basic problems, is a form of heartlessness and insincerity. With much reflection, prayer and study I reached the conclusion that practically every Birch program is the antithesis of Christianity.

Most importantly, the Birch Society wasn't hurting the Communist movement. Rather, it was promoting the idea that Communism was such a gigantic threat—all powerful, all-invincible, all successful in infiltrating every government in the world—that it was almost futile to even hope that we had a chance against it. The Birch line was so effective, in fact, that Welch's main problem these days is to convince the membership that all is not lost, that America still has a chance to preserve its freedom, if only it will unite behind the saving graces of Robert Welch.

As for escaping middle-class anonymity, mediocrity, conformism and meaninglessness, the plain truth finally dawned on me. Being different just for the sake of being different was not an achievement, but just an admission that perhaps I was inadequate to make my mark on the world through the normal channels of accomplishment. If I could not express my own individuality, if I could not find fulfillment and self-realization, if my job was a bore and my life was a waste, well, who's fault could that be but my very own?

These thoughts occupied my mind for months while I went through the motions of impeaching Earl Warren, getting the U.S. out of the United Nations, supporting our police, winning the war in Vietnam, abolishing the income tax and signing up new members to carry on the great Birch crusade. Finally, about the time an honest Negro forced me to come to grips with my own conscience, I decided I had to let go of Robert Welch's apron strings and begin to think and act for myself again. Birchism had been my business; but not for much longer.

I resigned soon after that. The reasons I gave were Belmont's refusal to allow me to weed the racists and anti-Semites out of the Society, the increasing incidence of defamation and foolishness at the national level and Robert Welch's personal failings which I could not live with any more.

It's not all that easy to return to normalcy after playing secret agent for two years. It's hard to get accustomed to living a routine life, devoid of publicity, verbal combat with "insidious enemies," and exciting sensations of being spied upon by agent provocateurs lurking on the other side of keyholes.

After leaving the Birch Society, I moved to the southwest Florida coast—the area I knew had the least number of Birch chapters. I settled down to a quiet life of teaching high school for the next two years.

Daily contact with teen-agers provided an excellent

177

opportunity to reexamine my ideas in a truly objective setting. Surprisingly, I discovered that a considerable number of students with middle-class upbringings held rigid opinions that were decidedly to the right of my own. I frequently assumed a liberal stance during classroom discussions just to maintain a balance of viewpoints.

A study of the Supreme Court convinced me that I preferred the court to err on the side of liberalism than endanger our personal freedom by granting too many powers to the central government. I still believe that the court often mistakes license for liberty, but this is preferable to leaning toward domestic totalitarianism.

I am much less concerned about threats from the United Nations. The United Nations, it seems to me, is an utter failure in its main purpose: to keep the peace of the world. In fact, it is shamefully irrelevant in that respect. But I suppose that it serves some purpose as a forum for international politicians to work off their frustrations in public. Also, United Nations social agencies make notable medical contributions in some areas of the world.

Leadership in parish youth activities exposed me to another element I had fought as a Birch coordinator. I got to know and greatly respect a number of people I worked with in a Mexican migrant-labor camp. The Birch position is that the attempt to organize migrant workers is another plot to start a Communist revolution in America. But anybody who meets these warm and long-suffering people, and sees the miserable conditions they are forced to live in through circumstances beyond their control, has to feel sympathy for their plight and shame that America—the land of opportunity—is apparently indifferent to this miserable cancer on its national sense of compassion and conscience.

Of course, I haven't given up all my conservative complaints. I can still get riled about galloping inflation and taxation. But then, not to complain about taxes would be downright un-American. As a former Bircher, I certainly wouldn't want to be accused of that.

It has not been easy to live down the atrocious reputation of the John Birch Society. Like a stubborn stain, it can't be rubbed off quickly. Perhaps this book will be my cleansing agent, and with the passage of time my error will become just another recollection in a life that has become well worth living.

Index

Index